Renal Diet

CookBook

The complete guide with low sodium and potassium recipes for a balanced and healthy diet with food tips to preserve your kidney

IRIS MOTLEY

Table of Content

Introduction

The human body has two kidneys. They're bean-shaped organs that reside on each side of the spine, just beneath the rib cage, in the back of the body. Each kidney is almost the same size as a fist. Your kidneys play a number of roles, the most important of which is to clean (filter) the blood, excreting toxins (waste), excess salt, & water as urine. If your kidneys are weakened and don't function as they should, waste can pile up in the blood and render you sick. Your kidneys help regulate the number of salts and minerals in the body, make hormones that regulate the blood pressure, create red blood cells and maintain your bones healthy.

Kidney disease suggests the kidneys have been damaged and aren't functioning as efficiently as they should. Kidney disease is referred to as "chronic" since kidney function deteriorates with time. Kidney disease proceeds to kidney failure, also known as end-stage renal disease. You'll either need dialysis (synthetic filtering) or a kidney transplant at this stage. Kidney disease is divided into five stages. The stages are determined by how effectively the kidneys filter waste and excess fluid from the blood. The stages range from the mildest (stage 1) to the most severe (stage 5) kidney failure (stage 5). The glomerular filtration rate is used by healthcare professionals to assess the stage of kidney activity (GFR). Chronic kidney disease (CKD) has no prevention, but early intervention may help to maintain a higher level of renal function for longer. If left untreated, absolute kidney failure can lead to death. Dialysis & kidney transplantation is two options for people with end-stage CKD. You may be given several medications based on the cause of the kidney disease.

A renal diet is a dietary program that is practiced to help reduce the number of waste materials in the blood. The renal diet is intended to inflict as little work or discomfort on the kidneys as feasible while also offering the energy and nutrients needed by the body. A renal diet adheres to a few basic principles. The first one is that it must be a well-balanced, nutritious, and long-term diet that is high in whole grains, vitamins, fibers, carbohydrates, omega-3 fats, and fluids. Proteins can be sufficient, but not extreme. Blood accumulates held to a basic minimum. Electrolyte levels in the blood are checked on a daily basis, and the diet is adjusted if required. It's important to meet the doctor's and dietitian's guidelines.

Protein consumption is essential to repair tissues on a daily basis, but it should be held to a basic minimum. The body must break down excess proteins into nitrates and carbohydrates. Nitrates are not used by the body and must be eliminated by the kidneys. Carbohydrates are a vital source of nutrition and should be consumed in sufficient quantities. Table salt should only be used in cooking. Excess salt induces fluid accumulation by overloading the kidneys. Diet is an essential aspect of CKD treatment, and it can significantly slow the disease's progression. There are foods that help your kidneys work, while some make your kidneys perform harder. You can feel like you're in the territory, unexplored, and navigating your needs may be difficult. To you and your family, all of the latest food do's, and don'ts can be puzzling at first; new dietary sometimes frustrating. One of the problems most kidney patients encounter is finding easy, nutritious CKD recipes to enable them to control the amounts of chemicals and fluids in their blood. This book aims to find a stable basis for experiencing the flavor of the food and making the right dietary adjustments.

Chapter 1: Understanding the Kidney Diseases

Kidney disease can impair your body's capacity to cleanse your blood, remove excess water from it, and regulate blood pressure. It may also have an effect on red blood cell development and vitamin D metabolism, all of which are essential for bone health. You have two kidneys from the time you are born. They are right above the waist, on each side of your spine.

Waste materials and fluid will persist in your body when the kidneys are affected. Swelling of the ankles, fatigue, exhaustion, bad sleep and difficulty breathing are also possible side effects. The damage could worsen without medication, and your kidneys can eventually stop functioning. That's a massive issue because it might put your life in jeopardy.

1.1 How the Kidneys Work?

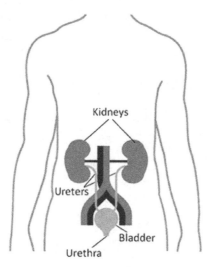

The two bean-shaped organs, each one about the size of the fist, are called kidneys. One on either side of the spine is found just under the rib cage.

Every minute, healthy kidneys process around a half cup of blood, extracting wastes and excess water to produce urine. Urine travels from the kidneys to the bladder along-with two thin muscle tubes known as ureters, one on either side of the bladder. Urine is stored in the bladder. The urinary system includes the kidneys, ureters, and bladder.

Your blood is filtered by two kidneys, which remove wastes and excess water to produce urine.

What is the significance of the kidneys?

Your kidneys are responsible for removing waste and excess fluid from the body. Your kidneys often filter out acid formed by your body's cells to keep a good balance of water, salts, and minerals in your blood, like sodium, calcium, phosphorus, and potassium. Nerves, muscles, as well as other tissues in the body, cannot function properly if this balance is not maintained.

Your kidneys also produce hormones that help:

- Control the blood pressure
- NIH external link to create red blood cells
- Keep the bones healthy and strong

What are the functions of the kidneys?

Around a million filtering units or nephrons are found in each of the kidneys. A filter is called the glomerulus, and a tubule is included in each nephron. The glomerulus cleans your blood, and the tubule restores needed substances to the blood, thus removing wastes.

The Nephron

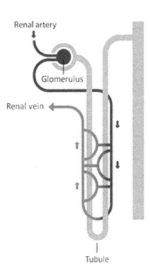

Each nephron has a glomerulus, which filters your blood, and a tubule, which returns required substances to your blood, thus removing waste. Urine is made up of waste and excess water.

Your blood is filtered by the glomerulus.

Blood enters a group of small blood vessels called the glomerulus as it passes through each nephron. Smaller compounds, wastes, and fluid—mostly water—can move through the glomerulus' thin walls and into the tubule. Proteins or blood cells, for example, are larger molecules that remain in the blood vessel.

The tubule extracts wastes and returns required compounds to your blood.

The tubule is flanked by a blood vessel. The blood vessel coagulates nearly all of the water, as well as the minerals and nutrients the body needs, as the filtered fluid flows through the tubule. The tubule succeeds in the removal of excess acid from the bloodstream. Urine is formed from the residual fluid and wastes in the tubule.

How is the blood flowing into the kidneys?

The renal artery is the blood vessel that supplies blood to the kidney. Until the blood enters the nephrons, this major blood vessel divides into progressively smaller blood vessels. The blood is filtered in the nephron through the glomeruli, which are small blood vessels, and eventually runs out of the kidney via the renal vein.

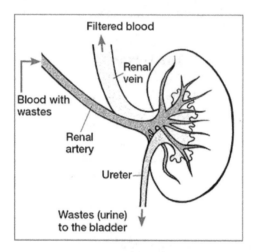

Your blood passes into the kidneys several times during the day. Your kidneys filter around 150 quarts of blood a day. Tubules return the majority of the water as well as other materials that filter into your glomeruli to your blood. Just 1 to 2 quarts of urine are excreted.

1.2 What Is Kidney Disease?

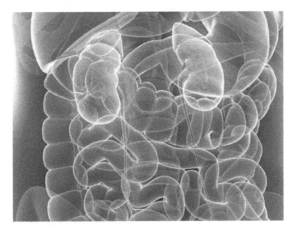

The kidneys are two fist-sized organs at the base of the rib cage. On either side of the spine, there is one kidney. A balanced body needs functioning kidneys. They remove waste material, extra

fluid, as well as other contaminants from the blood. Toxins are contained in the intestine and only excreted by urination. The body's pH, salt, & potassium levels are also controlled by the kidneys. They make hormones that govern the development of red blood cells and manage blood pressure.

Even a type of vitamin D that aids calcium absorption is activated by the kidneys. Kidney disorder impacts around 26 million people in the United States. It happens when your kidneys are weakened and unable to work properly. Diabetes, hypertension and a variety of other chronic (long-term) illnesses may all trigger damage. Kidney disease may result in brittle bones, nerve damage, and malnutrition, among other complications.

The kidneys may eventually stop functioning completely if the condition worsens. This suggests that dialysis would be required to fulfill the kidney's function. Dialysis is a medical procedure that uses a pump to clean and purify the blood. It will not treat kidney failure, but it will help you live longer.

Symptoms of Kidney diseases

The kidneys can respond to a variety of situations. They will help you deal with some of the issues that come with kidney disease. As a result, if the kidney damage proceeds progressively, the signs will appear gradually. In reality, signs cannot appear before the condition worsens.

You may have:

- Elevated blood pressure

- Vomits and nausea

- Loss in Appetite

- Metallic flavor in the mouth

- Tiredness

- Weakness

- Trouble in thinking

- Issues of sleep

- Muscle cramps and spasms

- Bruising of the ankles and feet

- Itching that doesn't seem to go anywhere

- Chest discomfort, as fluid builds up across the lining of the heart.

- Breathe shortness as the fluid piles up in the lungs.

1.3 Types of Kidney Diseases

CKD- Chronic kidney disease

Chronic kidney disease is the most prevalent form of kidney disease. A chronic kidney disorder is a long-term illness that does not get better. High blood pressure is a general factor.

High blood pressure can put too much pressure on the glomeruli in the kidneys, causing them to fail. Glomeruli are small blood vessels in the kidneys that clean the blood. The elevated pressure destroys these vessels over time, causing kidney function to deteriorate.

Kidney function will gradually deteriorate to the extent that the kidneys will be unable to function properly. Dialysis will be needed in this situation. Dialysis removes excess fluid as well as waste from the blood. Dialysis is a treatment for kidney failure, although it is not a solution. Depending on the situation, a kidney transplant might be an alternative.

Diabetes is also the primary source of chronic kidney disease. Diabetes is a category of disorders that trigger elevated blood sugar levels. Over time, the elevated sugar content in the blood affects the blood vessels in the kidneys. This indicates that the kidneys are unable to adequately cleanse the blood. When your body is polluted with contaminants, kidney failure may occur.

The term "chronic kidney disorder" refers to long-term kidney damage that can worsen over time.

Your kidneys can stop working if the disease is serious. Kidney failure, also known as end-stage renal disease, is a condition in which the kidneys stop working (ESRD). You may require dialysis or a kidney transplant to survive if the kidneys fail.

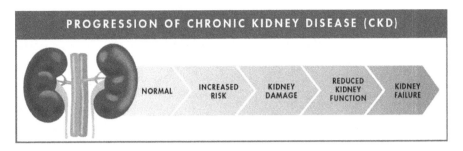

What induces chronic kidney disease (CKD) to develop?

CKD can affect everyone. Few people are in a higher danger than others. Some factors that raise the chances of developing CKD involve:

- Diabetes
- Blood pressure that is too high (hypertension)
- Cardiac disease
- To have a close relative with kidney disease
- To be American, Hispanic, African Native American, or Asian
- Being above the age of 60

What are the signs and indications of kidney disease?

If your kidneys are failing, you may experience several of the following symptoms:

- Itchy skin
- Muscle spasms
- Vomiting and nausea
- Not in the mood to eat
- Swelling of the ankles and foot
- There's either so much urine (pee), or there's not enough urine.
- Having difficulty catching the breath
- Sleeping problems

You can experience several of the symptoms listed if your kidneys cease to function unexpectedly (acute kidney failure):

- Pain in the abdomen (belly)

- Pain in the back

- Fever

- Diarrhea

- Rash

- The nose bleeds

- Vomiting

Facing one or more of the symptoms mentioned above may indicate severe kidney problems. If you have some of these signs, you should see your doctor as soon as possible.

Complications of Chronic Kidney Disease

Your kidneys support the proper functioning of the whole body. If you have CKD, you can have complications with the rest of your body's functioning. Anemia, bone disorder, cardiac disease, high potassium, high calcium, and fluid accumulation are all typical complications of CKD.

Stages of Chronic Kidney Disease

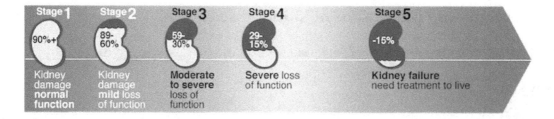

Chronic kidney disease (CKD) is a term that encompasses all five stages of kidney damage, ranging from minor damage in stage 1 to total kidney failure in stage 5. The kidney failure stages are determined by how effectively the kidneys filter waste and excess fluid from the blood. Your kidneys will also remove waste from the blood in the initial stages of kidney disease. Your kidneys will have to work harder to get rid of waste in the latter stages, and they can also stop working completely.

EGFR is a metric used by doctors to assess how effectively your kidneys absorb waste from your blood. Your estimated glomerular filtration rate (eGFR) is determined by a blood examination for creatinine, a waste substance in your blood.

The eGFR number is used to categorize kidney disease stages.

eGFR of 90 or greater indicates stage 1 CKD.

When you have stage 1 CKD, you have moderate kidney failure and an eGFR of Ninety or higher.

An eGFR of 90 or higher usually indicates that your kidneys are stable and functioning well, but you have other symptoms of kidney damage. Protein in the urine (pee) or physical damage to the kidneys are also signs of kidney damage. In Stage 1 kidney disease, there are a few things you should do to help slow down the risk to the kidneys:

- If you have diabetes, keep your blood sugar under control.

- Let the blood pressure check.

- Consume a balanced diet and refrain from smoking or using nicotine.

- Maintain a good weight by being active for 30 minutes five days a week.

- Consult the specialist to see if there are any medications that will better strengthen the kidneys.

- Even if you do have a general practitioner, schedule an appointment with a nephrologist (kidney specialist).

Stage 2 CKD: eGFR of 60 to 89 years old

If you have stage 2 CKD, you have minor kidney damage as well as an eGFR of 60 to 89.

An eGFR of 60 to 89 usually indicates that the kidneys are stable and functioning properly. However, even though your eGFR is fine, if you have Stage 2 kidney failure, you can show some symptoms of kidney damage. Protein in the urine (pee) or physical damage to the kidneys are also signs of kidney damage. In Stage 2 kidney disease, there are a few things you can do to help slow down the harm to the kidneys:

- If you have diabetes, keep your blood sugar under control.

- Keep your blood pressure in check.

- Consume a balanced diet and refrain from smoking or using nicotine.

- 30 minutes of physical activity, five days a week

- Maintain a good weight.

- Consult the specialist to see if there are any medications that will better strengthen the kidneys.

- And if you do have a general practitioner, schedule an appointment with a nephrologist (kidney specialist).

Stage 3 CKD: eGFR of 30 to 59 years old

If you have stage 3 CKD, the eGFR is between 30 and 59.

An eGFR of 30 to 59 indicates that the kidneys have been damaged and are not doing as well as they should.

Step 3 is divided into two sections:

- If your eGFR is between 45 and 59, you're in stage 3a.

- If your eGFR is between 30 and 44, you're in stage 3b.

Sometimes patients with kidney damage in Stage 3 don't have any signs or symptoms. However, if there are signs and indications, these may include:

- The hands and feet are swollen.

- Pain in the back

- More or less urinating (peeing) than normal

- When waste piles up in the body, and the kidneys fail to function properly, you're more likely to develop health problems, such as:

- Blood pressure that is too high

- Anemia (a lower amount of red blood cells)

- Bone disorder

You should do the following to prevent your Stage 3 kidney disease from becoming worse:

- If you have diabetes, keep your blood sugar under control.

- Keep your blood pressure in check.

- Smoking and tobacco consumption are not recommended.

- Maintain a balanced lifestyle.

- 30 min of physical activity, five days per week

- Maintain a good weight.

- Consult a nephrologist (kidney doctor), who can devise a medical plan tailored to your needs and advise you about how often your kidneys should be examined.

- Talk with a dietitian that will assist you with maintaining a balanced diet.

- If you have diabetes or elevated blood pressure, talk to a doctor about ACE inhibitors and ARBs, which are blood pressure medications. These medications may also help prevent kidney disease from worsening.

Stage 4 CKD: eGFR of 15 to 29 years old

If you have stage 4 CKD, the eGFR is between 15 and 29.

If your eGFR is between 15 and 30, your kidneys are mildly or seriously compromised and not functioning properly. Step 4 kidney disorder, which is the last stage prior to kidney failure, should be treated very seriously.

Some patients with stage 4 kidney disease experience signs such as:

- The hands and feet are swollen.

- Pain in the back

- More or less urinating (peeing) than normal

- As waste piles up in the body and the kidneys fail to function properly, you will possibly experience health risks at Stage 4, such as:

- Blood pressure that is too high

- Anemia (a lower amount of red blood cells)

- Bone disorders

- Your doctor will advise you to do the following to prevent kidney disease from worsening at this stage.

- Meet with a nephrologist (kidney doctor) on a regular basis, who will devise a treatment plan that is best for you and advise you how much your kidneys can be tested. Also, meet with a dietitian who can assist you with maintaining a balanced diet.

If the doctor recommends it, take blood pressure medications such as ACE inhibitors and ARBs. These drugs can also help prevent kidney failure from worsening whether you have diabetes or high blood pressure.

Now is the moment to start communicating to your nephrologist on how to brace for kidney failure if you have Stage 4 kidney disease. To survive when your kidneys malfunction, you'll need to start dialysis or get a kidney transplant.

Making preparations for dialysis: As your kidneys failed, dialysis cleans your blood. There are many factors to consider, including the form of dialysis, how to schedule the appointments, and how they can impact your everyday life.

Getting ready for a transplant: A kidney transplant is a procedure that replaces the damaged kidney with a healthy one from someone else's body. You do not need to begin dialysis at all if you can choose a compatible kidney donor. When your kidneys are on the verge of failing, you might be eligible for a transplant.

Stage 5 CKD: eGFR of fewer than 15

If you have stage 5 CKD, the eGFR is less than 15.

An eGFR of less than 15 indicates that the kidneys are on the verge of failing or have already failed entirely. Waste piles up in the bloodstream as the kidneys fail, making you really sick.

The below are some of the signs and symptoms of kidney failure:

- Itchy skin
- Muscle spasms
- Feeling unwell and throwing it up
- Not in the mood to eat
- The hands and feet are swollen.
- Pain in the back
- More or less urinating (peeing) than normal
- Breathing problems
- Sleeping problems

To survive when your kidneys failed, you'll need to start dialysis or get a kidney transplant.

Being ready for dialysis: When the kidneys fail, dialysis is used to clean your blood. There are many factors to consider, including the form of dialysis, how to schedule the appointments, and how they can impact your everyday life.

Being ready for a transplant: A kidney transplant is a procedure that replaces the damaged kidney with a healthy one from someone else's body. You do not need to begin dialysis at all if you can find a compatible kidney donor. If your kidneys are on the verge of failing, you might be eligible for a transplant.

Other kidney diseases

Stones in the kidneys

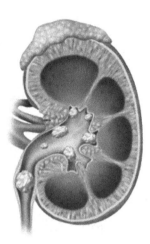

A kidney stone is another commonly affected condition. They arise as minerals as well as other compounds crystallize in the blood in the kidneys, creating hard masses (stones). Kidney stones are normally passed by the body through urination. Kidney stones may be excruciatingly painful to pass, but they seldom create serious complications.

Glomerulonephritis

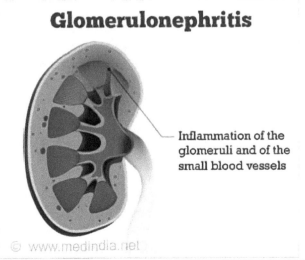

Glomerulonephritis

Inflammation of the glomeruli and of the small blood vessels

© www.medindia.net

Glomerulonephritis is a condition under which the glomeruli become inflamed. Glomeruli are tiny blood-filtering structures found within the kidneys. Infections, medicines, and congenital defects may all induce glomerulonephritis (disorders that occur during or shortly after birth). It usually improves on its own.

Polycystic kidney disease – PKD

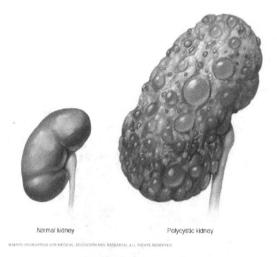

Normal kidney   Polycystic kidney

Polycystic kidney disease is an inherited condition in which the kidneys develop multiple cysts (small sacs of fluid). These cysts can cause kidney failure by interfering with kidney function. (It's worth noting that specific kidney cysts are relatively common and mostly innocuous.) Polycystic kidney disorder, on the other hand, is a different, more debilitating condition.)

Infections of the urinary tract

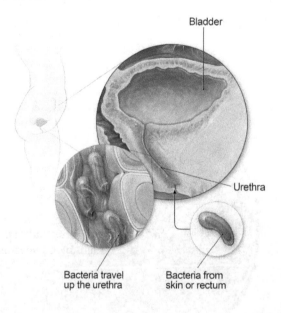

Bladder

Urethra

Bacteria travel up the urethra   Bacteria from skin or rectum

Urinary tract infections (UTIs) are infectious diseases of the urinary tract that may affect any part of the body. The most prevalent infections are those of the bladder and urethra. They are readily curable and rarely result in additional health issues. These diseases can occur to the kidneys and lead to kidney failure if left untreated.

1.4 Kidney Diseases Diagnoses

Your doctor can first assess whether you fall into either of the high-risk categories. They'll then do some examinations to see if the kidneys are in good working order. The following are examples of possible tests:

Glomerular filtration Rate (GFR)

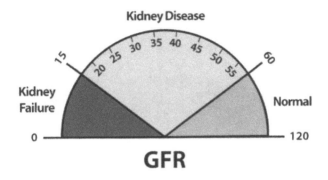

This check will assess the level of kidney failure and how well the kidneys are functioning.

Ultrasound or computerized tomography (CT) scan

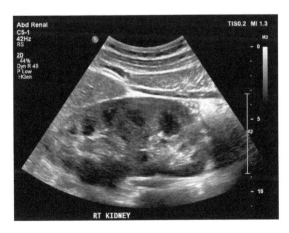

The kidneys & urinary tract can be seen clearly with ultrasounds & CT scans. Your doctor will use the photos to determine if the kidneys are too little or too large. They may even reveal any lesions or systemic issues that may exist.

A biopsy of the kidney is performed.

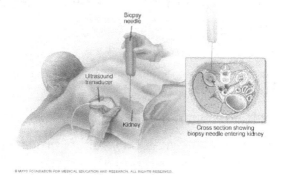

While you're sedated, the doctor will take a little piece of tissue from the kidney during a kidney biopsy. Your doctor will use the tissue sample to assess the type of kidney condition you have and the extent of the damage.

Urine examination

A urine test could be requested by your doctor to monitor for albumin. While your kidneys are affected, albumin is a material that can spill into your urine.

Creatinine level in the blood

Creatinine is a product of no use in our body. When creatinine (a molecule contained in muscle) is broken down, it is released into the blood. If the kidneys aren't functioning well, the amount of creatinine in the blood may increase.

What is the treatment for kidney disease?

Kidney disease treatment typically works upon fixing the disease's root cause. This ensures that the doctor can work with you to improve the way you control your blood pressure, sugar levels, & cholesterol levels. To control kidney disease, they can use either one of the following procedures.

Medication & Drugs

Angiotensin-converting enzyme (ACE) modifiers, like lisinopril & ramipril, or angiotensin receptor blockers (ARBs), irbesartan, and olmesartan, may be prescribed by the doctor. There are medicines for blood pressure, which may slow down kidney disease progression. Even if you don't have high blood pressure, your doctor can recommend these drugs to help you maintain kidney function. Cholesterol medicines can also be used to help you (such as simvastatin). These drugs can help sustain kidney health by lowering blood cholesterol levels. Your doctor can also recommend medications to alleviate swelling and cure anemia, depending on your symptoms (decrease in the number of red blood cells).

Changes in diet and lifestyle

It's just as necessary to make dietary adjustments as it is to take drugs. Many of the root factors of kidney disease may be avoided when adopting a healthier lifestyle. You might be advised by your doctor to:

- insulin injections for diabetes management
- Limit the intake of high-cholesterol items.
- cut back on salt
- start a heart-healthy diet that involves fresh fruits, veggies, whole grains, as well as low-fat dairy products
- limit your alcohol intake
- Do not smoke
- weight loss

Kidney disorder and dialysis

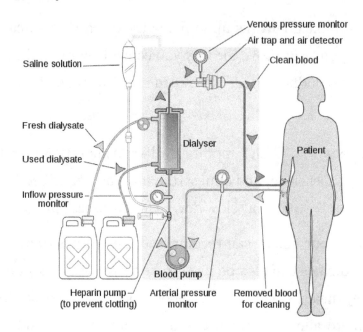

Dialysis is a means of filtering blood that is performed artificially. It's given when a person's kidneys have damaged or are on the verge of failing. Many patients with advanced kidney disease may undergo dialysis for the rest of their lives or before a donor's kidney can be identified.

Hemodialysis & peritoneal dialysis are the two forms of dialysis.

Hemodialysis

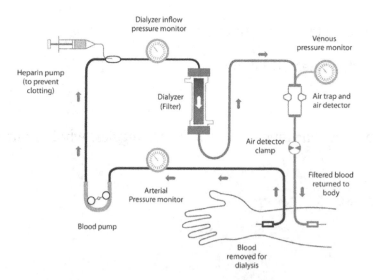

Hemodialysis involves pumping blood into a device that cleans out waste materials and excess fluid. Hemodialysis may be performed at home, in a hospital, or at a dialysis clinic. The average person has three sessions a week, each lasting 3 to 5 hours. Hemodialysis, on the other hand, should be performed in shorter, more regular sessions.

Most patients may undergo surgery to develop an arteriovenous (AV) fistula a few weeks before beginning hemodialysis. An AV fistula is formed when an artery, as well as a vein, is joined just under the skin, usually in the forearm. Through hemodialysis procedure, the broader blood vessel permits for more blood to circulate continuously across the body. More blood will be drained and cleaned as a result of this. Where an artery and vein cannot be linked, an arteriovenous patch (a looped, silicone tube) may be inserted and used for the exact reason. Low blood pressure, muscle pain, and itching are the most frequent hemodialysis side effects.

Peritoneal Dialysis

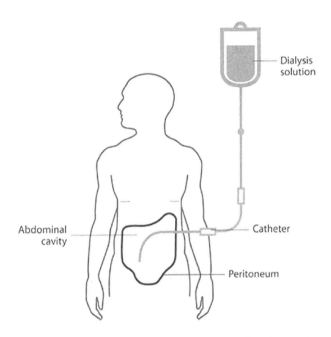

The peritoneum (abdominal wall membrane) serves as a substitute for the kidneys in peritoneal dialysis. A tube is inserted into the abdomen and used to cover it with a fluid called dialysate. Waste items of the peritoneum's blood flow through the dialysate. After that, the dialysate is extracted from the abdomen.

Continuous ambulatory peritoneal dialysis, in which the abdomen is filled and drained many times during the day, as well as continuous cycler-assisted peritoneal dialysis, in which a machine cycles the fluid in and out of the abdomen as the patient sleeps, are the two types of peritoneal dialysis. Infections in the abdomen or in the region where the tube was inserted are the most frequent adverse effects of peritoneal dialysis. Excess weight and hernias are two other possible side effects.

When the intestine tries to push into a sensitive point or tear in the bottom abdominal wall, it is called a hernia.

What is the prognosis for those with kidney disease in the long run?

When kidney disease is diagnosed, it usually does not go away. The easiest way to keep your kidneys healthy is to lead a healthy life and respond to your doctor. The condition of your kidneys can deteriorate over time. It may also result in kidney failure. If kidney failure is not treated, it may be deadly.

Kidney failure happens when the kidneys hardly function or don't work. Dialysis is used to manage this. Dialysis is the process of filtering waste from the blood using a machine. Your doctor may suggest a kidney transplant in certain instances.

How can you avoid kidney disease?

Most kidney disease risk factors, such as age, ethnicity, or family background, are uncontrollable. There are, though, things you may do to help mitigate kidney disease:

- Drink enough water
- When you have diabetes, keep your blood sugar under check and your blood pressure under control.
- Reduce salt consumption and stop smoking.
- Over-the-counter medicines should be used with caution.

For over-the-counter drugs, always observe the dose guidelines. Kidney damage may be caused by taking quite enough aspirin (Bayer) or ibuprofen (Advil, Motrin). If the usual dosage of these drugs isn't reducing the pain, see the doctor.

Examine yourself.

Demand a blood test for kidney complications from the doctor. Kidney conditions usually don't show signs until they've progressed. A basic metabolic panel (BMP) is a common blood test that may be performed as part of a regular medical examination. It looks for creatinine or urea in your blood. When the kidneys aren't functioning well, contaminants leak into the blood. A BMP can diagnose kidney disease early on when it's easiest to handle. If you have diabetes, heart disease, or elevated blood pressure, you should be tested every year.

Certain foods can be avoided.

Certain chemicals in your diet can play a role in the formation of kidney stones. There are some of them:

- Excessive sodium

- Animal protein, such as beef and chicken

- Citric acid, found in citrus fruits such as oranges, lemons, and grapefruits

- Oxalate, a chemical found in beets, spinach, sweet potatoes, and chocolate

1.5 Slowing the Kidney Disease

You are having the kidneys working, even if just a little, which will improve your health and make you live longer. You can defer the need for kidney disease treatment if you can slow down the CKD. Changes you make to support the heart or the rest of the body can often benefit your kidneys. Here are few measures you should do to secure your kidneys — or avoid.

Keep the blood sugar within the specified range.

Blood vessels, like the nephrons of the kidneys, become affected by high blood sugar. If you have diabetes, the doctor will set a fasting blood sugar limit for you and also a goal for 2 hours after you consume. Check your blood sugar levels frequently to see if they fluctuate depending on what you consume and how productive you are. If you haven't already done this, reduce your intake of added sugar and processed carbohydrates such as bread, desserts, and rice. Take a walk or engage in other forms of physical activity. Take your diabetes medication(s) exactly as directed.

Maintain the blood pressure in the specified range prescribed by your doctor.

Even if the blood pressure has always been normal, it can now be extreme — and difficult to manage. It is common for people with CKD to need several blood pressure medications. At home, check the blood pressure. Keep track of your readings so you can inform your doctor whether your blood pressure is high or low, even when you take the blood pressure medications. If you're experiencing adverse effects, consult with the doctor; a new medication may be best for you. Exercise may also assist in the reduction of blood pressure.

If you are overweight, you should lose weight.

The CARDIA analysis of young adults (average age 35) over a 10-year period discovered that the more people gained, the quicker their kidney function deteriorated. And if they didn't have

diabetes or elevated blood pressure, they became affected. It is difficult to lose weight. However, it is possible, and there are several methods that can be used. If you need guidance, ask the health practitioner for assistance.

Soda should not be consumed.

The consumption of one or two daily sodas a day has been attributed to kidney damage in a major study. A second major study discovered that drinking two or three diet sodas per day can cause kidney damage or hasten it.

Whether you smoke or use illicit drugs, make an effort to quit!

The kidneys are harmed by smoking and other street narcotics. Generally, if leaving were easy, everybody would do it. There are many methods for quitting smoking, including cold turkey, patches, nicotine gum, and e-cigarettes. And a reduction in the amount of food you eat can be beneficial. If you are using street drugs, you can need rehabilitation. If you require assistance quitting a habit that is causing you damage, talk to the healthcare staff.

Maintain a healthy pH level in your blood.

The pH in your blood may be 7.38 to 7.42. When the kidneys aren't working well, they can't hold the acid–base balance in the body in control. The acid will build up in your body as a result of eating protein-rich foods. Grains and protein items such as meat, poultry, dairy, beans, or peas break down into acid wastes. Protein is required by the body for muscle repair and self–repair. However, most of us consume much more protein than we require. One strategy to make your kidneys work longer, at least whether you're aged, is to eat a low-acid diet (with plenty of vegetables). Ask your doctor whether sodium bicarbonate will also actually shield your kidneys. It is really low cost and functions in tablet shape.

Reduce the protein intake.

Blood urea nitrogen is generated as protein is broken down (BUN). The kidneys get a difficult time eliminating BUN. When you consume less protein, you produce less BUN, which will extend the life of your kidneys. According to research, consuming a relatively low protein diet may improve much better. However, this is difficult to do — because there is a chance of deprivation.

Phosphorus should be avoided at all costs.

Meat, poultry, seafood, dairy, nuts, beans, and cola beverages all contain phosphorus. Your kidneys aren't removing as much phosphorus from the blood as they should be. Your bones will become brittle if the levels are too high.

Shellfish can be consumed in moderation.

In mice, researchers discovered that a toxin named domoic acid present in shellfish and certain fish that consume algae would damage the kidneys. Human beings are not mice. The most alarming result was that even extremely low amounts of the toxin would damage the kidneys. Purines are common in shellfish, which may be problematic if you have gout. If you consume a lot of shellfish, it may be a good idea to cut down.

Don't eat canned foods.

Bisphenol A is used to line most food cans (BPA). Hypertension, diabetes, and obesity have also been related to BPA. Often packaged foods are rich in salt or sugar, as well as highly processed. BPA is not used in glass jars or shelf-stable cartons.

Specific pain relievers should be avoided.

NSAIDs (nonsteroidal anti-inflammatory drugs) may damage the kidneys. To function properly, the kidneys need a steady flow of blood. Blood flow into and out of kidneys is reduced by NSAIDs. In most instances, NSAIDs induce CKD after years of everyday use. However, once CKD has developed, NSAIDs can hasten its progression. Consult the doctor for pain relief choices that aren't harmful to the kidneys. If you take one pill every now and then and your kidneys are still functioning, follow that up with a complete glass of water.

Do you want an X-ray with a contrast dye?

Inquire for Kidney Precautions. An MRI or CT scan dye that is pumped through a vein can move into the kidneys. Gadolinium is a pigment that can damage the kidneys. This dye may also induce a condition known as nephrogenic systemic fibrosis, which is an unusual condition (NSF). NSF thickens the skin and organs, and it may be lethal. NSF may not provide treatment. If your doctor recommends an X-ray dye examination, find out if there are any other options for learning the same details.

Antioxidants May Be Beneficial.

Every cell in the body requires oxygen to function properly. However, so much oxygen in the wrong places can trigger damage, similar to rust. Antioxidants strengthen your cells and can even benefit your kidneys. Consult the doctor and see whether antioxidants like these are beneficial. Fish oil may help reduce the progression of CKD induced by IgA nephropathy. Before taking every

supplement, vitamin, or over-the-counter remedy, consult the healthcare provider. When the kidneys aren't working well, they will build up in the body to dangerous levels.

Get moving

Heart failure and stroke are also linked to CKD. Diseases that affect the kidneys also affect the heart and blood vessels as well. The positive thing is that moving keeps your blood moving, which benefits the heart and kidneys by the blood flow. As a result, exercising is a win–win situation for the health. It can also slow the progression of CKD. Each day, aim for 30 minutes of physical movement. And, all of these 30 minutes don't have to happen at once. If you choose, you can divide your workout into 10–minute sections.

Are you thinking of beginning a workout routine?

If it's been a long time since you've exercised, see your doctor first. Begin slowly and gradually increase time, distance, or weight. Keep track of your results to see how you're going. You may also set objectives for yourself and encourage yourself as you achieve them.

Exercise does not even have to consist of a monotonous jog on a treadmill at a high-priced gym. Here are few more ideas to consider, and you may come up with much more of your own:

Walking is excellent exercise, and if you walk with a partner, you can spend time together as well. You should go on a stroll outside if the weather is good and you live in a secure area. Alternatively, often people walk in malls or at indoor tracks to avoid missing out. You'll get a more vigorous exercise if you jog–walk (alternating between jogging and walking).

Pick a sport to participate in. If you like a competitive activity, such as bowling, tennis, or badminton, you will share time with others while still improving your health.

Do some kind of work. Paint the wall or the fence. Pick any herbs or cut the grasses in the backyard. Use a push mower to mow the grass. Vacuum a few of the spaces. You'll accomplish everything, feel positive about yourself, and be productive as a participant.

Dance, Skate, and Have Fun. Moving is moving, whether you're jumping on a trampoline, paddling a canoe, or taking your buddy for a spin. Consider what you enjoyed as a child; it will inspire you to try new stuff.

Chapter 2: Understanding the Renal Diet

A renal diet is a dietary program that is practiced to help reduce the number of waste materials in the blood. The renal diet is intended to inflict as little work or discomfort on the kidneys as feasible while also offering the energy and nutrients needed by the body. A renal diet adheres to a few basic principles.

2.1 What Is A Renal Diet?

People with impaired kidney function should stick to a kidney or kidney diet to reduce the level of waste in the blood. Food & liquids ingested are the sources of wastes in the body. The kidneys do not filter or extract waste adequately while their function is compromised. The electrolyte concentrations of a patient will be affected if waste is stored in the blood. A kidney diet can also help to improve kidney function and stop the growth of kidney failure.

The renal diet is deficient in sodium, Phosphorus as well as protein. A renal diet emphasizes the value of eating high-quality protein and, in certain cases, restricting fluids. Potassium and calcium restrictions could be needed for certain patients. Since each patient's body is specific, it's important that they interact with a renal nutritionist to create a diet that's personalized to their specific needs.

Some compounds to keep an eye on to maintain a renal diet are mentioned below:

Sodium

What exactly is sodium, and what role does it have in the human body?

Sodium is a substance that can be present in a wide variety of foods. The majority of people confuse sodium and salt. However, salt is simply a product of sodium and chloride. Salt or sodium in many other forms can be present in the foods we consume. Owing to the addition of salt, processed foods frequently have higher sodium levels. One of the three main electrolytes of the human body is sodium (potassium & chloride are the other two). The fluids that enter and exit the body's cells and tissues are regulated by electrolytes. Sodium plays a role in the following processes:

- Keeping blood pressure & blood volume in check

- The function of nerve and muscular contractions is controlled.

- Keeping blood's acid-base balance in check

- Keeping the body's fluid intake and secretion in check

Why is it essential for kidney patients to keep track of their sodium consumption?

Since their kidneys cannot properly remove excess sodium as well as fluid from the body, too much sodium may be dangerous to those with kidney disease. The accumulation of sodium and fluid in the tissues & bloodstream will result in:

- An increase in thirst

- Edema: swelling of the thighs, hands, and face.

- Hypertension

- Failure of heart: surplus fluid in the bloodstream can overstress your heart, making it bloated and weak.

- Breathing difficulties: fluid can accumulate in the lungs, rendering breathing difficult.

What are the best ways for patients to keep track of their sodium consumption?

- Always read indications on food. The amount of sodium in a product is always defined.

- Keep an eye on the portion sizes.

- Instead of packaged meats, use fresh meats.

- Choose fresh fruit and vegetables or non-salt-added canned and frozen items.

- Don't eat anything processed.

- Compare products to find the lowest sodium options.

- Use spices whose names do not include the word "salt" (choose garlic powder rather than garlic salt.)

- Do not use salt while cooking at home.

- Total sodium intake does not exceed 400 mg per meal or 150 mg per snack.

Potassium

What is potassium, and what part does it have in the human body?

Potassium is a substance that can be present in a variety of foods as well as in the human body. Potassium helps to maintain the heartbeat normal and the muscles in good working order. Potassium is often needed to keep the bloodstream's fluid and electrolytes balanced. The kidneys assist in maintaining a healthy potassium balance in the body by excreting extra potassium into the urine.

Why is it essential for kidney patients to keep track of their potassium intake?

As the kidneys weaken, the body's potassium levels rise since the kidneys are unable to remove extra potassium. Hyperkalemia is a condition in which there is so much potassium in the blood, which may lead to:

- Muscle weakening

- A heartbeat that is abnormal

- A slow heartbeat

- Having a heart attack

- Death

How do patients keep track of their potassium consumption?

When the kidneys can no longer control potassium, a patient's potassium intake must be monitored.

Keep the following in mind to help keep the potassium levels in check:

- Make an eating plan with the help of a renal dietitian.

- Potassium-rich foods should be avoided.

- Limit yourself to 8 ounces of milk and dairy items a day.

- Fresh fruits & vegetables are the best choices.

- Potassium-containing seasonings and salt equivalents should be avoided.

- Avoid potassium chloride by reading the warnings on processed goods.

- Keep an eye on the serving amount.

- Keeping a food diary is a good idea.

Phosphorus

What is Phosphorus, and what function does it have in the human body?

Phosphorus is an essential mineral for bone health and growth. Phosphorus is also essential for the growth of interconnected tissue and organs, as well as the movement of muscles. When phosphorus-rich food is eaten and digested, the Phosphorus is absorbed by the small intestines and retained in the bones.

Why is it essential for kidney patients to keep track of their Phosphorus intake?

Additional Phosphorus in the blood will be removed by normal functioning kidneys. As kidney functioning is affected, the kidneys are unable to extract extra Phosphorus from the body. High phosphorus levels will reduce calcium in your bones, causing them to become brittle. Calcium concentrations in the blood vessels, lungs, eyes, as well as heart, become toxic as a result of this.

How will patients keep track of their Phosphorus consumption?

Phosphorus is used in a variety of foods. As a result, patients with impaired kidney function must see a renal nutritionist help them balance their phosphorus levels.

- Learn which foods have a lower phosphorus content.

- Keep a careful eye on the serving amount.

- At meals and snacks, consume smaller amounts of high-protein items.

- Fresh vegetables and fruit should be consumed.

- Consult the doctor on the use of phosphate binders during mealtime.

- Phosphorus-fortified processed foods should be avoided. On ingredient labels, look for Phosphorus or terms that start with the letters "PHOS."

- Hold a food diary.

Protein

Protein is not an issue for kidneys in good health. Protein is usually ingested, and waste materials are produced, which are then removed by the kidney's nephrons. The waste is then converted to urine with the aid of certain renal proteins. Damaged kidneys, on the other hand, fail to eliminate protein waste, which builds up in the blood. Protein intake is difficult for Chronic Kidney Disorder patients, and the amount varies depending on the level of the disease. Protein is necessary for tissue preservation and other bodily functions, but follow your nephrologist's or renal dietician's recommendations for your particular level of disease.

Fluids

Fluid management is critical for patients with Chronic Kidney Disease in the later stages because regular fluid intake can lead to fluid buildup in the body, which can be harmful. Excessive fluid in the body may place undue pressure on a dialysis patient's heart and lungs since their urine output is also reduced.

The fluid amount for each patient is determined by his or her urinary production and dialysis settings. It's important to stick to the nephrologist's/fluid nutritionist's intake recommendations.

To keep their fluid consumption under check, patients should:

- Drink just as much as the doctor prescribes.

- Count up all the foods that would melt when left out at room temperature.

- Keep track of the number of fluids you use while cooking.

2.2 Foods to Eat and Avoid On Renal/Kidney Diet

Renal Diet Foods to **Eat** and **Avoid**

Bel Marra Health

The kidneys are tiny organs just below the abdomen which play an important role in the body's overall health. Some foods can help the kidneys perform better, while others can put them under stress and inflict damages.

Waste material from the blood is filtered by the kidneys and excreted in the urine. They are often in need of maintaining fluid and electrolyte balance.

These functions are carried out entirely by the kidneys. Diabetes and elevated blood pressure are two conditions that may hinder their ability to work.

Damage to the kidneys will eventually contribute to chronic kidney disease (CKD). Diet is the most relevant risk factor for CKD-related sickness and death, according to the writers of a 2016 study, rendering dietary adjustments an essential aspect of recovery.

A kidney-friendly diet can help the kidneys work better and avoid harm to these vital organs. However, while certain diets are beneficial to a stable kidney, not all of them are appropriate for people with kidney disease.

Water

The essential liquid for the body is water. Toxins are transported into the blood by cells using water.

Water is then used by the kidneys to filter such toxins and produce urine, which carries them out of the bloodstream.

Drinking if an individual is thirsty will help to sustain these functions.

Fatty Fish

Salmon, tuna, or other cold-water fatty fish with significant omega-3 fatty acid content may be a healthy addition to every diet. Omega-3 fatty acids are not produced by the body, so they must be ingested by food. Healthy fats can be found in abundance in fatty fish.

Omega-3 fats can lower blood pressure and reduce fat levels in the blood, according to the National Kidney Foundation. Seeking natural ways to reduce blood pressure, which is a potential risk for kidney disease, can actually shield the kidneys.

Sweet potatoes

Sweet potatoes are identical to white potatoes, but because of their high fiber content, they can break down more slowly, leading to a lower insulin spike. Sweet potatoes even contain vitamins and minerals, like potassium, that can help to stabilize sodium levels in the body and lessen the kidney's effect.

Sweet potato is a high-potassium item, so those with CKD or on dialysis can restrict their consumption.

Dark leafy greens

Dark leafy greens, including spinach, kale, and chard, are food staples that are high in vitamins, fiber, and minerals. Antioxidants and other protective substances are used in many of them.

However, since these items are rich in potassium, they might not be safe for those on a limited diet or others who are on dialysis.

Berries

Dark berries, such as strawberries, blueberries, including raspberries, are high in nutrients, minerals, and antioxidant compounds. These can help to protect the body's cells from damage. Berries are probably to be a safer option for soothing a sweet tooth than most other sugary foods.

Apples

An apple is a nutritious snack that includes pectin, a form of fiber. Pectin can assist in the reduction of certain kidney-damaging risk factors, such as hypertension as well as cholesterol levels. Apples are indeed a great way to satisfy a sugar craving.

Foods to stay away from

If people wish to strengthen their kidney function or minimize risk to these organs, they must avoid a few foods.

The following are some of them:

Foods that are high in Phosphorus

The kidneys may be stressed with so much Phosphorus. High phosphorous consumption has been linked to an elevated risk of kidney damage in the long run, according to research. However, there is insufficient evidence to demonstrate that phosphorous triggers this effect, requiring further study.

Foods rich in phosphorous include:

- Meat
- Dairy
- A lot of grains
- Legumes
- Nuts

- Fish

- Red meat

Some proteins are more complex for the kidneys, or the body as a whole, to digest. Red meat is one of them.

People who consume a lot of red meat have a greater chance of end-stage kidney disease than someone who eats less red meat, according to preliminary reports. However, further research is needed to fully understand this hazard.

Foods to eat if you have CKD

Although the foods mentioned above may promote kidney health in general, they are not always the top options for people with CKD. Many patients with CKD would be placed on a special diet to prevent nutrients processed by the kidneys, like sodium, potassium, even phosphorous.

People with CKD can consume fewer than 2,300 milligrams of sodium a day, according to the National Institute of Diabetes and Digestive and Kidney Diseases. People with CKD may need to restrict their phosphorous consumption when the disease progresses, as this mineral may mount up in the blood of those that have it.

Potassium amounts that are too high or too low may cause complications in people with CKD, so choosing the correct amount is crucial. People with CKD can consume a variety of healthy foods that are low in these minerals but high in other nutrients. People with CKD can often need to limit their protein consumption and only have minimal quantities of protein in their meals. Protein is converted to waste by the body, which must be filtered out by the kidneys.

According to a 2017 report, consuming a low-protein diet can protect against CKD complications, including metabolic acidosis that arises as kidney function declines. According to the researchers, a diet high in fruits and vegetables and low in protein can help to reduce these risks.

People with CKD should consult closely with a dietitian to develop a diet plan that is appropriate for them.

Cabbage

Cabbage is a greenery vegetable that can help people with kidney disease. While it is limited in potassium and sodium, it provides a variety of beneficial compounds &

Vitamins.

Bell peppers, red

Red bell peppers produce beneficial antioxidant compounds that may protect cells from a concussion, in addition to being low in minerals like sodium and potassium.

Garlic

For people with CKD, garlic is an outstanding seasoning choice. It will offer other foods a richer, more pleasing taste, potentially reducing the need for excessive salt. Garlic also has a number of nutritional advantages.

Cauliflower

Cauliflower is a nutritious vegetable for patients with chronic kidney disease (CKD). It may be used as a substitute for rice, mashed potatoes, or even pizza crust when prepared properly.

Cauliflower seems to have a variety of nutrients without a lot of sodium, potassium, and phosphorous.

Arugula

Most vegetables are off-limits to people with CKD, but arugula is a perfect substitute. While arugula has a lower potassium content than other greens, it still provides fiber and other nutrients.

Berries

Patients with CKD can enjoy blueberries as a healthy snack.

For people with CKD, the fruits mentioned below may be a healthy sweet snack:

- Cranberries
- Strawberry
- Blueberries
- Raspberry
- Grapes (red)
- Cherries
- Olive oil

Because of the type of fat it produces, olive oil might be the best cooking oil. Olive oil is rich in oleic acid, a polyunsaturated fatty acid that can aid in the reduction of inflammation.

Whites of eggs

Eggs are a basic protein with a high phosphorous content in the yolks. Egg whites can be used to make omelets or fried eggs for people with CKD.

Foods to skip if you have CKD

Any foods can be challenging for people with CKD to digest, putting more strain on the kidneys. There are some of them:

- Potatoes

- Red meat

- Dairy goods

- Beverages that are high in sugar

- Avocado

- Bananas

- Foods in cans

- Foods that have been pickled

- Alcohol

- yolks of eggs

Eat these foods in moderation if you want to preserve your kidneys from future damage.

Conclusion

Filtration of the blood and elimination of waste materials in the urine are essential functions of the kidneys. Many foods can help protect a kidney that is already balanced and remove the risk to it. Individuals with chronic kidney disease, on the other hand, may need to adhere to a different range of dietary guidelines in order to preserve their kidneys from more damage.

Before making any dietary changes, it's certainly a good thing to consult with a certified dietitian.

Chapter 3: The Renal/Kidney Diet Recipes

3.1 Breakfast Recipes

1. EASY TURKEY BURRITOS

Serving: 8

Preparation time: 30 minutes

Nutritional values: Sodium-513mg|Potassium-285mg|Phosphorus-359mg|Protein-25mg|Carbs-23g|Fat-24g

Ingredients

- 1 pound ground turkey or surplus turkey meatloaf, cubed thin 8-inch flour burrito shells

- a 1/4 cup of canola oil

- 8 poached eggs, beaten

- a quarter-cup of onions, chopped

- 1/4 cup chopped red, yellow, or green bell peppers

- 2 tbsp. jalapeno peppers, seeded

- 2 tbsp. diced fresh scallions

- 2 tbsp. chopped fresh coriander

- 1/2 tsp. chili powder

- 1/2 tsp. paprika (smoked)

- 1 cup Monterey Jack & Cheddar cheese, shredded

Directions

1. In half the oil, sauté the meatloaf, onions, onions, scallions, and coriander unless fluorescent. Mix in the spices, then remove from the flame.

2. Set a moderate flame in a separate wide sauté pan and add the residual oil and poached eggs.

3. Fill burrito shells with equal quantities of vegetable & meatloaf mixture, cheese, as well as eggs, then roll & serve.

2. BLUEBERRY MUFFINS

Serving: 12

Preparation time: 35 to 45 minutes

Nutritional values: Sodium-210mg|Potassium-121mg|Phosphorus-100mg|Protein-5g|Carbs-44g|Fat-9g

Ingredients

- 1/2 cup butter (unsalted)

- A quarter cup of sugar

- Two eggs

- 2 cups 1% of the milk

- 2 cups flour (all-purpose)

- Baking powder, 2 tsp.

- 1/2 tsp. of salt

- 2 1/2 cup blueberries, fresh

- Sugar (two tsp.) (for sprinkle)

Directions

1. Blend the margarine & sugar together at low speed unless smooth and fluffy.

2. Mix in the eggs one at a moment unless well mixed.

3. Trawl the dry ingredients and alternate adding them with the milk.

4. Mash ½ cup of blueberries and mix by hand. Then, by hand, bring in the leftover blueberries.

5. Spray the muffin cups and the tray with vegetable oil on the surface. In a muffin tin, arrange the muffin cups.

6. Fill each muffin cup to the maximum with a muffin mixture—top muffins with sugar.

7. Preheat oven to 375°F and bake for 25–30 minutes. Allow cooling for at least 30 min in the pan before carefully extracting.

3. STUFFED BISCUITS

Serving: 12

Preparation time: 40 minutes

Nutritional values: Sodium-330mg|Potassium-152mg|Phosphorus-170mg|Protein-11g|Carbs-19g|Fat=23g

Ingredients

- Flour (two cups)

- 1 tbsp. of sugar (or honey)

- 1/2 tsp. of baking soda

- 1 tbsp. of lemon juice

- 8 tsp. of unsalted softened butter, tempered

- 3/4 cup of milk

Stuffing/Filling:

- Four eggs

- 8 oz. lowered -sodium bacon (11/4 chopped)

- 1 cup of chopped Cheddar cheese

- 1/4 cup of finely diced scallions

Directions

1. Preheat the oven to 425 degrees Fahrenheit.

Filling Preparation:

1. Underdone poached eggs

2. Crisp up the bacon in a skillet.

3. Combine the four ingredients in a mixing bowl and set aside.

Dough Preparation:

1. Integrate all dry ingredients in a big mixing bowl.

2. With a fork or a pastry knife, cut in unsalted butter until pea-size or less.

3. Make a well in the middle of the mixture, then knead in the milk and lemon juice.

4. Use a lining or gently grease & dust the bottom and sides of muffin tins.

5. Fill muffin tins with 1/4 cup of batter.

6. Preheat oven to 425°F and bake for 10-12 minutes, or until lightly browned.

4. FLUFFY HOMEMADE BUTTERMILK PANCAKES

Serving: 9

Preparation time: 15- 22 minutes

Nutritional values: Sodium-330mg|Potassium-182mg|Phosphorus-100mg|Protein-6g|Carbs-27g|Fat-9g

Ingredients

- 2 cups flour (all-purpose)

- 1 tsp. Tartar cream

- a total of 11/2 tsp. baking soda

- 2 spoonful's of sugar

- 2 cups buttermilk (low-fat)

- 2 eggs, large

- 1 tbsp. canola oil and 1/4 cup canola oil (for cooking)

Directions

1. Preheat a skillet over medium-high heat.

2. In a wide mixing bowl, incorporate the dry ingredients. Integrate the dry ingredients with the buttermilk, oil, and egg in a mixing bowl. Mix the dry ingredients with a wand or a spoon until they are fully moist.

3. Grease the pan with a tbsp. of canola oil. Scrap the pancake batter into the skillet using a 1/3-cup measuring cup. Thus every pancake should have a wingspan of around 4 inches. For effective flipping, leave around 2" between the pancakes. Flip pancakes with a spatula once the bubbles on the surface have mostly vanished. Make the other side be colored until it no longer looks moist in the middle.

4. Transfer to a serving tray.

5. Consider eating with fresh berries as well as a side of eggs for a healthy twist.

5. CHEESESTEAK QUICHE

Serving: 6

Preparation time: 1hr 10min

Nutritional values: Sodium=392mg|Potassium-308mg|Phosphorus-281mg|Protein-22g|Carbs-22g|Fat-19g

Ingredients

- 1/2 lb. coarsely cut sliced sirloin steak

- 1 cup diced onions

- 2 tbsp. oil (canola)

- 1/2 cup shredded pepper jack cheese

- 5 pounded eggs

- 1 cup of cream

- 1" x 9" prepared deep par-cooked piecrust*

- 1/2 tsp. black pepper, ground

Directions

1. Make coarse pieces out of the shaved sirloin.

2. In a frying pan with oil, brown the sliced steak as well as onions until the meat is cooked. Allow cooling for 10 minutes. Enable to sit after folding in the cheese.

3. In a wide mixing bowl, whisk together the eggs, milk, and black pepper unless completely combined.

4. Place the steak and cheese mixture on the bottom of the par-cooked piecrust, then add the egg mixture on top and cook for 30 minutes at 350° F.

5. Turn off the oven and cover the cheesesteak quiche with foil. Allow for a 10-minute cooling period before serving.

6. SPICY TOFU SCRAMBLER

Serving: 2

Preparation time: 20 minutes

Nutritional values: Sodium-24mg|Potassium-467mg|Phosphorus-242mg|Proteins-18g|Carbs-10g|Fat-13g

Ingredients

- 1 tsp. of olive oil
- 1/4 cup sliced red bell pepper
- 1/4 cup chopped green bell pepper
- 1 cup tofu (firm) (choose less than 10 percent calcium)
- 1 tsp. powdered onion
- ¼ tsp. of garlic powder
- 1 garlic clove, finely chopped
- 1/8 tsp. turmeric

Directions

1. Sauté the garlic and both bell peppers in olive oil in a standard size fry pan.
2. Wash and drain the tofu and corrode it in the pan. Integrate the rest of the ingredients and stir well.
3. Mix and cook on low - to - medium flame until the tofu becomes golden brown, around 20

minutes. The water in the mixture will evaporate.

4. Serve the scrambler tofu warm.

7. SOUTHWEST BAKED EGG BREAKFAST CUPS

Serving: 12

Preparation time: 1hr

Nutritional values: **Sodium-79mg|Potassium-82mg|Phosphorus-91mg|Protein-5g|Carbs-13g|Fat-4g**

Ingredients

- 3 cups cooked rice

- 4 oz. sliced cheddar cheese

- 4 oz. sliced green chilies

- 2 oz. washed and chopped pimentos

- 1/2 cup of skim milk

- 2 beaten eggs

- 1/2 tsp. cumin powder

- 1/2 tsp. black pepper

- Cooking spray, which is nonstick

Directions

1. Rice, 2 ounces cheese, chilies, milk, eggs, pimentos, cumin, and pepper should all be mixed together in a large mixing bowl.

2. Use the nonstick cooking spray to coat muffin cups.

3. Fill 12 muffin cups equally with the mixture—the remaining 2 oz. Shredded cheese can be sprinkled on top of each cup.

4. Preheat oven to 400°F and bake for 15 minutes, or until fixed.

8. CAULIFLOWER ASPARAGUS TORTILLA

Serving: 1-4

Preparation time: 45 minutes

Nutritional values: Sodium-248mg|Potassium-472mg|Phosphorus-97mg|Protein-9g|Carbs-9g|Fat-3g

Ingredients

- 2 cups sliced asparagus (bite-size pieces)

- 2 cups of cauliflower, diced in pieces of bite-size.

- 2 teaspoons extra virgin olive oil

- 1 1/2 cups finely minced onion

- 1 clove of garlic, chopped

- 1 cup liquid low-cholesterol egg substitute

- 2 tbsp. thinly sliced fresh parsley

- Salt (1/4 teaspoon)

- 1/2 teaspoon pepper, freshly ground

- 1/4 tsp. crumbled dry thyme leaves

- 1/4 tsp. nutmeg powder

Directions

1. In a microwave-safe, covered dish, add the asparagus & cauliflower pieces with 1 tablespoon water. Steam for 3 to 5 minutes in the microwave before crisp and tender.

2. Simmer the onion for around 7 minutes, or until golden.

3. Cook for 1 minute further, stirring constantly.

4. Integrate the asparagus, egg substitute, parsley, salt, cauliflower, pepper, thyme, and nutmeg in a large mixing bowl.

5. Reduce heat to low and cook, covered, for 10 to 15 minutes, or until set and golden brown on the bottom.

6. Invert onto a heated platter or serve straight from the skillet after softening the edge with a knife.

9. BAGEL WITH SALMON AND EGG

Serving: 1-2

Preparation time: 20 minutes

Nutritional values: Sodium-378mg|Potassium-338mg|Phosphorus-270mg|Protein-19g|Carbs-29g|Fat-14g

Ingredients

- Half bagel
- 1 tbsp. of cream cheese
- Scallions, 1 tbsp.
- 1/2 tsp. dill (fresh)
- 2 basil leaves, fresh
- 1 tomato slice
- Arugula (four pieces)
- 1 large egg

1 oz. salmon cooked

Directions

1. Cut the bagel into half and toast half of it in a toaster or oven.
2. Cut the scallions, dill, and basil leaves into small pieces. Mix well with the cream cheese.
3. Cover the toasted bagel half with the cream cheese mixture, arugula, and a tomato slice.
4. Fumble the egg in a frying pan sprayed with nonstick spray.
5. While the egg is cooking, braise the salmon in a similar pan.

6. On top of the tomato slice, place the egg and salmon. Have fun.

10. CLASSIC EGGS BENEDICT

Serving: 4

Preparation time: 40 minutes

Nutritional values: Sodium-346mg|Potassium-174mg|Phosphorus-214mg|Protein-16g|Carbs-14g|Fat-35g

Ingredients

- 4 oz. sliced Canadian bacon

- Three cups of water (divided use)

- 2 muffins (English)

- 1 tbsp. of vinegar

- 4 eggs

- Half-cup of unsalted butter

- 3 beaten egg yolks

- Cayenne powder, a pinch

- Pinch of paprika

- 1 tbsp. of lime juice

Directions

1. Put the Canadian bacon in 2 cups boiling water for five min to de-mineralize it.

2. Using a slotted spoon, remove the chicken and place it on top of some paper towels to drain the moisture. English muffins should be halved and toasted.

3. Put half of the Canadian bacon on top of every toasted muffin half.

4. In a deep pan, mix vinegar and around one cup of sugar. Bring to a simmer, then switch off the heat.

5. Poach the eggs one at a time by cracking them and slipping them into the water—cover and cook for 3 to 5 minutes, or until eggs are cooked to your preference.

6. With a slotted spoon, remove the eggs and put them on top of the bacon & English muffin; wrap and keep it warm.

7. Melt the butter

8. Over low heat, whisk the egg yolks.

9. Add the melted butter, paprika, and cayenne pepper to the pan quickly.

10. Mix in the lime juice until it becomes thick.

11. Remove the pan from the heat and pour over the English muffins.

11. CHILLED SUMMER SQUASH AND TURMERIC SOUP

Serving: 1

Preparation time: 40 minutes

Nutritional values: Sodium-279mg|Potassium-504mg|Phosphorus-138mg|Protein-4g|Carbs-10g|Fat-5g

Ingredients

- 4 cups of low sodium vegetable stock

- Two medium squash of zucchini

- Two medium yellow crook-neck squash

- One tiny onion

- 1/2 cup of thawed green peas

- 2 tbsp. of olive oil

- 1/2 tsp. of kosher salt

- Half cup plain Greek yogurt

- 2 tsp. of turmeric

Directions

1. Cut the zucchini, the yellow squash, and the onion into huge chunks.

2. Take the stock to a boil in a saucepan, then minimize heat to medium heat.

3. Mix in the zucchini, the yellow squash, and the onion and boil for 25 minutes.

4. Cook for an extra 5 minutes after adding the green peas, oil, and salt.

5. Allow the soup to cool to room temperature after removing it from the heat.

6. To make a smooth consistency, mix the ingredients together in a blender. Combine the Greek yogurt with turmeric in a mixing bowl.

7. Refrigerate for at least six hours or overnight while eating chilled soup.

12. ASPARAGUS AND CHEESE CREPE ROLLS WITH PARSLEY

Serving: 1

Preparation time: 1hr 8min

Nutritional values: Sodium-247mg|Potassium-357mg|Phosphorus-142mg|Protein-10g|Carbs-16g|Fat-24g

Ingredients

- 12 spears of asparagus

- Cream cheese, 4 oz.

- 1 parsley bundle

- Lime juice (1 teaspoon)

- Black pepper, 1/2 tsp.

- 1/3 cup flour (all-purpose)

- 1/2 cup of water

- Cream, 1/4 cup

- 1 beaten egg

- Two egg whites

- Butter (four tbsp.)

Directions

1. Heat the asparagus for six to eight minutes.

2. To make a green cream sauce, puree cream cheese with parsley, lime juice, and spices. Season to taste. Let it away.

3. To create crepes, whisk together the flour, water, egg, egg white, and two tablespoons melted butter unless creamy.

4. In a skillet (8 to a 10-inch crepe or frying pan), melt half a tablespoon of butter. Pour in 1/3 cup crepe batter and rotate pan to evenly distribute batter. Cook until the mixture is bubbling and the sides are beginning to brown. Cook for a few minutes, on the other hand. Place on a plate to cool. To create four crepes, repeat with the remaining butter and batter.

5. Spread cream cheese filling on crepes. At the end of each crepe, evenly divide the asparagus spears and tightly fold them up into rolls.

6. Refrigerate for 1 hour after wrapping in foil. Before eating, cut cooled crepes into 3-4 sections with a sharp knife.

3.2 Lunch Recipes

1. KNOCK –YOUR-SOCKS-OFF CHICKEN BROCCOLI STROMBOLI

Serving: 4

Preparation time: 40 minutes

Nutritional values: Sodium-607mg|Potassium-546mg|Phosphorus-400mg|Protein-38g|Carbs-52g|Fat-17g

Ingredients

- 1 pound pizza dough (bought from the store)

- 2 cups broiled fresh broccoli florets

- 2 cups cooked chicken breast, finely chopped

- 1 cup lower-salt mozzarella cheese, sliced

- 1 tbsp. minced fresh garlic

- 1 tbsp. chopped oregano

- 1 tsp. red pepper flakes, squashed

- Flour (two tablespoons)

- 2 tbsp. extra virgin olive oil

Directions

1. Preheat the oven to 400 degrees Fahrenheit.

2. In a wide mixing bowl, incorporate the chicken, pepper flakes, cheese, broccoli, garlic, and oregano.

3. Dust the counter with flour and cut out the dough into an 11" x 14" shape.

4. Along the longest side of the dough, put the chicken mix around 2 inches from the edge.

5. Roll and push the ends and seams together until they are fully closed

6. Brush the upper part of the dough with olive oil and cut three narrow slits in it.

7. On a lightly greased baking sheet pan, bake 8–12 min or until lightly browned.

8. Remove from the oven and set aside for 3–5 minutes before slicing and serving.

2. COOL AND CRISPY CUCUMBER SALAD

Serving: 4

Preparation time: 2hrs

Nutritional values: Sodium-74mg|Potassium-90mg|Phosphorus-14mg|Protein-0g|Carbs-3g|Fat-2g

Ingredients

- 2 cups of fresh cucumber (peeled and diced into 1/4-inch slices)

- 2 tbsp. salad dressing (Italian or Caesar)

- To taste freshly roasted black pepper

Directions

1. Integrate cucumber as well as a salad dressing in a medium-sized bowl with a lid.

2. Move to coat and cover with a lid.

3. Season with freshly ground black pepper. Keep refrigerated.

4. It's best eaten cold.

3. SMOKY & SAVORY SALMON DIP

Serving: 12

Preparation time: 30 minutes

Nutritional values: Sodium-147mg|Potassium-259mg|Phosphorus-110mg|Protein-10g|Carbs-2g|Fat-9g

Ingredients

- 1 pound of fresh, skinless salmon sliced into four pieces.

- 2 tsp. of smoked paprika

- 1 cup of cream cheese

- ¼ cup of the capers

- ¼ cup of lime juice and half a lime zest (around 1 tsp.)

- 2 tsp. of red onions, thinly chopped

- 1 tsp. of ground black pepper

- 1 tbsp. fresh parsley snipped

Directions

1. Poach the salmon in 2 cups of water as well as 1 tsp. Of smoked paprika about 4–6 minutes on moderate flame; cover the pot, but do not boil. Remove and refrigerate for at least thirty min.

2. Mix all the other components together until the mixture is smooth. Split salmon into small bits and fold into a combination of cream cheese.

3. Allow 20–30 minutes for the salmon dip to chill. Serve with celery, corn chips, and carrots, or wrap in an iceberg lettuce leaf.

4. HERB ROASTED CHICKEN BREASTS

Serving: 4

Preparation time: 2hr 15min

Nutritional values: Sodium-53mg|Potassium-491mg|Phosphorus-252mg|Protein-26g|Carbs-3g|Fat-17g

Ingredients

- 1-pound chicken breasts (boneless and skinless)

- 1 onion, medium

- A couple of garlic cloves

- Mrs. Dash® Garlic & Herb Seasoning Mix (two tablespoons)

- 1 tsp. black pepper, ground

- 1/4 cup extra virgin olive oil

Directions

Preparation:

1. Place the onion and garlic in a bowl and chop them up. Add Ms. Dash Seasoning, ground pepper as well as olive oil.

2. Refrigerate the chicken breasts for about 4 hours or overnight after adding them to the marinade.

Baking Instructions:

1. Preheat oven to 350 degrees Fahrenheit (180 degrees Celsius).

2. Put the chicken breasts that were marinated on a baking sheet covered with foil.

3. Bake the chicken for 20 minutes at 350°F with the leftover marinade.

4. For browning, broil for another 5 minutes.

5. EGG FRIED RICE

Serving: 10

Preparation time: 20-30 minutes

Nutritional values: Sodium-38mg|Potassium-89mg|Phosphorus-67mg|Protein-5g|Carbs-21g|Fat-4g

Ingredients

- 2 tsp. of sesame oil (dark)

- Two eggs

- 2 beaten egg whites

- 1 tbsp. canola oil

- 1 cup of bean sprouts

- 1/3 cup chopped green onions

- 4 cups frozen cooked rice

- 1 cup thawed frozen peas

- 1/4 tsp. black pepper, ground

Directions

1. In a medium bowl, whisk together the sesame oil, eggs, and egg whites. Set aside after thoroughly stirring.

2. In a wide nonstick skillet, heat up canola oil over moderate flame.

3. Stir in the egg mixture until it is completely cooked.

4. Add the green onions and bean sprouts. Stir-fry for a couple of minutes.

5. Toss in the rice & peas. Stir-fry until it is fully cooked.

6. Serve right after seasoning with black pepper.

6. THREE-PEA SALAD WITH GINGER AND LIME DRESSING

Serving: 6

Preparation time: 20-25 minutes

Nutritional values: Sodium-70mg|Potassium-117mg|Phosphorus-40mg|Protein-3g|Carbs-6g|Fat-21g

Ingredients

- Sugar snap peas, 1 cup

- 1 cup peas (snow peas)

- 1 cup of sweet peas, fresh or chilled frozen

Vinaigrette:

- 1 tsp. low sodium soy sauce

- 1/4 cup lime juice, freshly squeezed

- 1 tsp. lime zest (fresh)

- 2 tsp. minced fresh ginger

- 1/2 cup canola olive oil

- 1 tbsp. sesame oil (hot)

- Sesame seeds, 1 tbsp.

- Freshly crushed rough pepper (black pepper) as per taste as an optional garnish

Directions

1. Slightly sauté the seeds of sesame in a hot frying pan for 4 to 6 min, flipping continuously.

2. Blanch all three varieties of peas for two min in a wide pot of boiling water at high temperature, rinse, and shock in a pot of ice water. Fill a strainer halfway with water and rinse thoroughly.

3. Whisk together the soy sauce, pepper, lemon juice, and zest in a small bowl until well combined, around one to two minutes.

4. Add the ginger and let them whisk. Steadily simmer in canola or grape seed oil, then incorporate the oil of sesame, stirring until well blended.

5. Integrate the dressing for salad and pea mixture in a wide mixing bowl. Shove with the seeds of sesame and season with black pepper to taste.

7. LEMON ORZO SPRING SALAD

Serving: 4

Preparation time: 45 minutes

Nutritional values: Sodium-79mg|Potassium-376mg|Phosphorus-134mg|Protein-6g|Carbs-28g|Fat-22g

Ingredients

- Orzo pasta (3/4 cup or 1/4 box)
- 1/4 cup chopped fresh yellow peppers
- 1/4 cup chopped fresh red peppers
- 1/4 cup diced fresh green peppers
- 1/2 cup Vidalia or red onion, minced
- 2 cups medium-cubed fresh zucchini
- 1/4 cup plus 2 tbsp. olive oil
- 3 tbsp. freshly squeezed lime juice
- 1 tsp. zest of lemon
- 3 tbsp. Parmesan cheese, grated
- Two tablespoons sliced fresh rosemary
- 1/2 tsp. black pepper
- 1/2 tsp. oregano, dry

- 1/2 teaspoon crushed red pepper

Directions

1. Process orzo pasta as directed on the package, then drain and set aside. (Refrain from rinsing.)

2. In a large skillet, sauté peppers, onions, and zucchini with 2 tablespoons oil over a moderate flame until crispy.

3. In a large mixing bowl, combine the lemon juice, lemon zest, 1/4 cup olive oil, cheese, pepper, rosemary, oregano, and red pepper flakes.

4. Fold the sautéed vegetables as well as orzo pasta together gently in a wide mixing bowl until well combined.

5. Serve chilled or at ambient temperature.

8. TURKEY STUFFED ZUCCHINI

Serving: 1

Preparation time: 1hr 15min

Nutritional values: Sodium-263mg|Potassium-578mg|Phosphorus-240mg|Protein-18g|Carbs-60g|Fat-11g

Ingredients

- 1/3 cup of onion
- 1/2 cup of mushrooms (button)
- 1 clove of garlic
- 3 zucchini (medium)

- Marinara sauce (about 3/4 cup)

- 1 tbsp. extra virgin olive oil

- 1 pound turkey (ground)

- 1 tsp. Italian seasonings

- Mozzarella cheese, 1/3 cup

- 2 tbsp. bread crumbs (panko)

Directions

1. Preheat the oven to 375 degrees Fahrenheit.

2. Cut the onion & mushrooms into small pieces. Garlic should be minced. Cut the ends of the zucchini and cut it in half stacked.

3. To make zucchini boats, scrape the internal flesh from the zucchini with a spoon edge. Remove the flesh and put it aside.

4. In a 13 x 9-inch baking tray, position zucchini boats, cover with aluminum foil and bake for 20 minutes or until fork ready.

5. Remove the zucchini from the oven and set aside to cool slightly.

6. Put olive oil in a skillet over the moderate flame while the zucchini is cooking. In an oven, combine the ground turkey, onion, and garlic. Stir until the ground turkey is fully cooked, splitting it up if required. Drop the extra grease.

7. In a pan, combine the zucchini flesh, marinara sauce, mushrooms, and Italian seasoning. To integrate, stir all together thoroughly—Cook for fifteen min on medium heat.

8. Squeeze turkey mix into zucchini boats that have been partially cooked. Wrap in foil and bake for twenty minutes.

9. Remove the foil and sprinkle mozzarella cheese & panko bread crumbs on top of the zucchini. Bake for an extra 3 to 5 minutes on the top rack of the oven, just before the cheese starts to brown. Remove the dish from the oven and enjoy.

9. PORK TENDERLOIN SWEET POTATO HASH

Serving: 3-4

Preparation time: 25 minutes

Nutritional values: Sodium-62mg|Potassium-448mg|Phosphorus-224mg|Protein-22g|Carbs-11g|Fat-8g

Ingredients

- 2 sweet potatoes, medium

- 1/2 yellow onion, medium

- 1 green onion, chopped

- 2 cups pork tenderloin, roasted

- 1 tbsp. extra virgin olive oil

- 1 tsp. of cinnamon

Directions

1. Sweet potatoes can be peeled and diced into 1/2-inch chunks. Half an onion and the green onion should be diced. Dice the pork loin that has been cooked.

2. Braise sweet potatoes twice. Put chopped sweet potatoes in a bowl with enough water to cover them completely. After bringing the water to a simmer, drain it. Cover the pot with water and bring it to a boil for ten min. remove the potatoes from the water.

3. Heat the olive oil in a pan over the moderate flame as the potatoes are cooking. Sauté the onion for five minutes.

4. Mix in the cinnamon with the potatoes.

5. Add the cooked sweet potatoes and the remaining pork to the pan and mix thoroughly for 3 to 4 minutes. Cook until the potatoes are finely browned if desired.

6. Serve with a green onion garnish. Have fun!

10. ALL AMERICAN MEATLOAF

Serving: 1-6

Preparation time: 50 minutes

Nutritional values: Sodium-299mg|Potassium-255mg|Phosphorus-14 7mg|Protein-17g|Carbs-14g|Fat-9g

Ingredients

- 2 tbsp. of onion

- 20 squares of saltine crackers (tops unsalted)

- 1 pound of lean beef (10 percent fat)

- 1 large egg

- 2 tbsp. 1% of low-fat milk

- 1/4 tsp. of black pepper

- 1/3 cup of catsup

- 1 tbsp. of brown sugar

- 1/2 tsp. of apple cider vinegar

- 1 tsp. of water

Directions

1. Preheat the oven to 350 degrees F.

2. Chop the onion finely. Put crackers in a big zip-top bag and smash them with a rolling pin.

3. Coat the loaf pan with a non - stick cooking spray on it.

4. In a large bowl, incorporate smashed crackers, onion, milk, beef, eggs, and black pepper. Mix nicely,

5. Place the mixture in the loaf pan—Bake for about 40 minutes.

6. Add catsup, brown sugar, vinegar & water in a small bowl to yield the topping.

7. Remove the baked meatloaf from the oven and coat it with the mixture.

8. Return the tray to the oven and bake for ten min or until the core temperature is 160°F.

9. Slice and serve in 6 pieces.

11. CHICKEN PASTA WITH BRUSSELS SPROUTS

Serving: 1-3

Preparation time: 30 minutes

Nutritional values: Sodium-228mg|Potassium-416mg|Phosphorus-217mg|Protein-20g|Carbs-19g|Fat-11g

Ingredients

- Green onions (half cup)

- 1/2 cup red pepper, sweet

- 1 1/2 cups Brussels sprouts (fresh or frozen)

- 1 1/2 cups whole wheat rotini pasta, cooked

- 1 tbsp. unsalted butter

- 1 tbsp. oil (canola)

- 1 tbsp. soy sauce (low sodium)

- 1 1/2 cups cubed cooked chicken

Directions

1. Cut the green onions & red peppers into small pieces.

2. Trim the Brussels sprouts' ends and boil or steam them until they are almost soft.

3. Cook pasta as per box instructions, obfuscating the salt.

4. Drain the Brussels sprouts and put them aside as the pasta cooks.

5. In a pan, melt oil and butter, then sauté green onions.

6. Stir in the red peppers & Brussels sprouts until they are just golden around the edges.

7. Add the soy sauce and cover the vegetable mixture before the pasta is done.

8. If necessary, reheat the chicken in the microwave.

9. In a mixing bowl, add the pasta, chicken, and cooked vegetables.

10. Serve when hot.

12. CHICKEN SQUARES

Serving: 1

Preparation time: 30-40 minutes

Nutritional values: Sodium-509mg|Potassium-210mg|Phosphorus-174mg|Protein-18g|Carbs-23g|Fat-22g

Ingredients

- 3/4-pound bone-in chicken breasts with skin

- Cream cheese, 3 tbsp.

- 1 tbsp. butter (unsalted)

- Broccoli florets, 1/2 cup

- 1 pack Crescent Original® Pillsbury rolls

Directions

1. Preheat the oven to 350 degrees Fahrenheit. Enable cream cheese to soften. Melt the butter in a skillet.

2. Broccoli should be cooked, drained, and chopped.

3. Steam chicken breasts until cooked through; drain, detach skin and bones, and dice.

4. Integrate the chicken, whipped cream cheese, melted butter, and broccoli in a mixing bowl.

5. Shape a rectangle with two crescent rolls by opening them up. To secure and stretch the rectangle, pinch the seam.

6. Make a turnaround by placing 1/4th of the chicken mixture in the middle and folding the sides over. To secure the sides, press them together.

7. Bake for 25–30 minutes until the rolls are golden brown.

3.3 Dinner Recipes

1. PESTO-CRUSTED CATFISH

Serving: 6

Preparation time: 30 minutes

Nutritional values: Sodium-272mg|Potassium-576mg|Phosphorus-417mg|Potein-26g|Carbs-15g|Fat-16g

Ingredients

- Catfish weighing 2 lbs. (boned and filleted) 6 bits of 5-ounce

- Pesto (four tsp.)

- Bread crumbs (panko): 3/4 cup

- 1/2 cup cheese (mozzarella)

- 2 tbsp. extra virgin olive oil

- Chef McCargo's Exclusive Seasoning Mixture:

- 1 tsp. powdered garlic

- 1 tsp. powdered onion

- 1/2 tsp. oregano, dry

- 1/2 tsp. crushed red pepper

- 1/2 tsp. black pepper

Directions

1. Preheat the oven to 400 degrees Fahrenheit.

2. In a small bowl, combine all of the seasonings and start sprinkling evenly on both sides of the fish.

3. Set aside equivalent quantities of pesto (1 tsp. each) on the topsides of the filets.

4. Mix the cheese, oil, and bread crumbs in a medium dish, then dredge the pesto side of the fish in the paste until well covered.

5. Put fish pesto side up on a baking sheet tray that has been liberally greased or sprayed with oil, leaving room between filets.

6. On the bottom rack, roast for 15 to 20 min at 400° F or unless optimal brownness is achieved.

7. Allow for a 10-minute rest period after extracting the fish from the tray to keep the fish from fracturing.

2. SMOKING CHICKEN WITH MUSTARD SAUCE

Serving: 8

Preparation time: 2hr 15min

Nutritional values: Sodium-300mg|Potassium-471mg|Phosphorus-278mg|Protein-28g|Carbs-9g|Fat-23g

Ingredients

- 2 lb. chicken breast, sliced thinly (or skinless and boneless chicken breast pounded thin)
- 1/4 cup shallots, finely chopped
- 1/4 cup sliced fresh scallions
- 1/2 cup flour
- 1/2 cup canola oil
- 2 cups chicken broth (less sodium)
- 1 tablespoon Chicken Base Better Than Bouillon® (low sodium)
- 2 tbsp. mustard (brown)
- 1/2 oz. unsalted butter, cubed and cooled

Seasonings:

- 1/2 tsp. black pepper
- 1/2 teaspoon seasoning (Italian)
- 1 tbsp. parsley, dry
- 1 tbsp. paprika (smoked)

Directions

1. In a small bowl, integrate pepper, Italian seasoning, paprika, and parsley.

2. Half of it goes on the chicken breast, and the rest goes in the flour.

3. In a wide sauté pan over medium-high heat, heat the oil.

4. Set aside three tablespoons of the prepared flour.

5. Cook for 2–3 min on either side after dredging the chicken in the leftover seasoned flour.

6. Remove the chicken from the pan and place it on a plate to cool. Remove everything except a few tbsp. Of the oil, incorporate the shallots and simmer until slightly opaque.

7. Whisk in the flour until smooth, then steadily add the stock when whisking. Reduce heat to low and mix in mustard, chicken bouillon, and unsalted butter after five minutes of cooking on a moderate flame.

8. Switch off the heat and return the chicken, along with any juice drippings from the plate, to the tray, stirring constantly. Serve with scallions as a garnish.

3. SPICY GRILLED PORK CHOPS WITH PEACH GLAZE

Serving: 8

Preparation time: 1hr 10min

Nutritional values: Sodium-158mg|Potassium-363mg|Phosphorus-188mg|Protein-23g|Carbs-27g|Fat-18g

Ingredients

- Eight 4-ounce center-cut pork chops (choose boneless pork chops)

- 1 cup of peach extracts (store-bought)

- 2 tsp. of coriander

- 1/4 cup of lemon juice and zest of 1 lemon

- 1 tbsp. of reduced-sodium soy sauce

- 1 tsp. of smoked paprika

- 2 tsp. of onion flakes, dry

- 1/2 teaspoon of red pepper flakes

- 1/2 teaspoon of black pepper

- 1/4 cup of olive oil

Directions

1. Heat the grill or turn on the electrical griddle to a high temperature.

2. Combine all the ingredients (except pork chops) in a small bowl until well blended.

3. Remove a quarter of the mixture and set aside and place the leftover marinade in a sack of pork chops & marinate for four hours (overnight would be better).

4. Grill pork chops for about 6–8 minutes on either side.

5. Glaze one more time before pulling from the grill and let it sit on the plate or platter for 7 to 10 min while serving.

4. GOONCHI AND CHICKEN DUMPLINGS

Serving: 10

Preparation time: 40 minutes

Nutritional values: Sodium-121mg|Potassium-485mg|Phosphorus-295mg|Protein-28g|Carbs-38g|Fat-10g

Ingredients

- 2 lb. breast of chicken

- Gnocchi (1 pound) (bought from the store)

- 1/4 cup mild olive oil or grape seed oil

- 1 tablespoon Chicken Base Better Than Bouillon® (low sodium)

- 6 cups chicken broth (low sodium)

- 1/2 cup finely chopped fresh celery

- 1/2 cup finely chopped fresh onions

- 1/2 cup finely chopped fresh carrots

- 1/4 cup minced fresh parsley

- 1 tsp. freshly ground black pepper

- 1 tsp. Italian seasonings

Directions

1. Place the stockpot on the stovetop, add the oil, and turn the heat up to maximum.

2. Cook the chicken in a hot skillet until lightly brown on both sides.

3. Proceed to cook with the chicken until the celery, carrots, and onions are translucent. Cook for 20 to 30 min on high heat with chicken stock.

4. Reduce the heat to low, then add in the chicken bouillon, black pepper, and Italian seasoning. Cook, stirring continuously, about 15 minutes after adding the gnocchi.

5. Take off from the heat, garnish with parsley, and serve.

5. BOURBUN - BLAZED SKIRT STEAK

Serving: 8

Preparation time: 35-40 minutes

Nutritional values: Sodium-152mg|Potassium-283mg|Phosphorus-171mg|Protein-24g|Carbs-8g|Fat-22g

Ingredients

Bourbon glaze:

- 1/4 cup shallots, finely chopped

- 3 tbsp. unsalted butter, cubed and chilled

- 1 cup of bourbon

- 1/4 cup sugar (dark brown)

- 2 tbsp. Mustard, Dijon

- 1 tablespoon freshly ground black pepper

Skirt Steak:

- Grape seed oil, 2 tbsp.

- 1/2 tsp. oregano, dry

- 1/2 tsp. paprika (smoked)

- 1 tsp. freshly ground black pepper

- 1 tbsp. vinegar (red wine)

- Skirt meat, 2 lb.

Directions

Bourbon glaze:

1. In a wide saucepan over a moderate flame, brown the shallots in 1 tbsp. Of butter.

2. Lower the heat to a minimum, remove the skillet from the flame, incorporate bourbon, and put the saucepan again on the stove.

3. Process for 10 to 15 min, or unless around one-third is reduced.

4. Bring brown sugar, mustard & black pepper and mix until bulbous.

5. Turn the heat off and whisk in the residual 2 tbsp. Of cold, diced butter, mixing vigorously until well blended.

Skirt steak:

1. Mix the first five ingredients in a gallon-sized sealed plastic container, add the steaks, and rattle well.

2. Enable steaks to soak in a bag at ambient temperature for 30-45 minutes.

3. Take the steaks from the container, grill for 15-20 minutes on either side, then take out and let stay for ten min.

4. Cut and serve with a mist of sauce, or end up leaving whole and dust with glaze and place in a preheated skillet for 4–6 minutes or until desired.

6. POT PIE CHICKEN STEW

Serving: 8

Preparation time: 50 minutes

Nutritional values: Sodium-424mg|Potassium-209mg|Phosphorus-290mg|Protein-26g|Carbs-22g|Fat-21g

Ingredients

- 1½ pounds of "natural" fresh boneless and skinless chicken breast

- 2 cups of reduced-sodium chicken stock

- ¼ cup of canola oil

- ½ cup of flour

- ½ cup of fresh carrots, chopped

- ½ cup of fresh onions, chopped

- ¼ cup of fresh celery, diced

- ½ tsp. of black pepper

- 1 tablespoon of free of sodium Italian seasoning

- 2 tsp. of Chicken Base (reduced sodium)

- ½ cup of fresh iced sweet peas, toasted.

- ½ cup of heavy cream

- 1 cooked iced piecrust, cut into bite-size portions
- 1 cup of low-fat Cheddar cheese

Directions

1. To tenderize the chicken, pound it and slice it into cubes.

2. Put chicken as well as stock in a wide saucepan and medium heat for thirty min. In the meanwhile, syndicate the oil & flour unless well combined.

3. Then drain slowly and stir in a mixture of chicken broth until it is lightly thickened. Lower the heat to minimal or medium heat for fifteen minutes.

4. Add onions, carrots, black pepper, celery, Italian seasonings, and bouillon. Cook for another fifteen min.

5. Turn off the heat, then bring the peas and the cream. Mix unless well balanced. Serve in mugs and fill with fair quantities of cheese and piecrust as a seasoning.

Substitute preparation of the crockpot:

1. Set the crockpot to the maximum for four hours.

2. Add the oil and simmer carrots, onions, and celery for around 5 minutes or until they are translucent.

3. Add flour and whisk until the paste starts to form, stirring continuously for around 3 minutes.

4. Incorporate chicken, black pepper, seasoning (Italian), and stock. Mix until well blended.

5. Cover and let it simmer, mixing about once an hour. Stir in the cream and peas about a half-hour before the end of the cooking time. Cover and stir regularly for the last thirty min of preparation.

6. Top with slices of piecrust and cheese to serve.

7. BBQ SAUCE-LESS BABY BACK RIBS

Serving: 12

Preparation time: 3 hours

Nutritional values: Sodium-102mg|Potassium-453mg|Phosphorus-198mg|Protein-18g|Carbs-33g|Fat-15g

Ingredients

- 2 slabs (approximately 3 1/2 lbs.) ribs from the baby back

- 12 mini-ears fresh or frozen corn on the cob

- 1 segment of the rub

- BBQ Spice Rub by Chef McCargo (combine all ingredients):

- 1 cup dark brown sugar, packed

- 1 tsp. freshly ground black pepper

- 1 tsp. crushed red pepper

- 1 tsp. paprika (smoked)

- 2 tsp. garlic granules = substitute Powdered garlic

- 2 tsp. onion flakes (dehydrated)

- 2 tsp. chili powder

Directions

1. Preheat the oven to 400 degrees Fahrenheit.

2. Spread the rub mixture evenly over both slabs of ribs.

3. Place the ribs on a tray lined with wire racks. Wrap securely with aluminum foil and cook for 11⁄2 to 2 hours.

4. Take out from the oven, then remove the foil. Set the ribs aside with tongs. Remove the ribs from the tray and drain the contents from the pan.

5. Cook for another 15 minutes or until the required texture is achieved.

6. Leave for 5 to10 min to rest period before cutting and serving.

7. Using a 9" x 9" microwave oven-safe pan to microwave the corn on the cob. In the dish, arrange both of the mini-ears of corn on their ends. Fill the dish with around 12 inches of water. Wrap the plastic wrap around the dish firmly. Microwave on maximum for 5–7 minutes.

An alternative to cooking on the grill:

1. To avoid burning, incremental cooking in a BBQ pit is advised.

2. For the first 3 hours, cook the ribs at 250° F (curled side up), then raise the heat to 300° F for the last 3 hours.

3. Remove the husk and any residual silk strands from each ear of corn before grilling it. Cover the corn in the foil of aluminum and barbecue for around 25 minutes, rotating periodically, until the corn is soft.

8. ROASTED GARLIC AND CRANBERRY RISOTTO

Serving: 3-4

Preparation time: 45 minutes

Nutritional values: Sodium-100mg|Potassium-184mg|Phosphorus-66mg|Protein-8g|Carbs-43g|Fat-7g

Ingredients

- Onion (1 cup)

- 2 tbsp. unsalted butter

- 3 tbsp. garlic, roasted

- 3/4 cup uncooked Arborio rice

- 2 cups chicken stock (low sodium)

- 1/2 cup dried cranberries, sweetened

- 1/2 tbsp. Parmesan cheese

Directions

1. Preheat the oven to 425 degrees Fahrenheit. Using nonstick cooking spray, coat a casserole dish.

2. Chop the onion finely.

3. In a wide saucepan, melt the butter. In a saucepan, mix the roasted garlic and onion and simmer over medium heat until tender.

4. Cook for 2 minutes after adding the rice.

5. Bring broth and dry cranberries to a mixture of rice. Bring to a boil, then reduce to a simmer for 2 minutes.

6. Pour the mixture into a casserole bowl—Bake for 30 minutes with the cover on.

7. Remove the dish from the oven and top with Parmesan cheese. Serve right away.

9. CREAMY ORZO AND VEGETABLES

Serving: 3-4

Preparation time: 20 minutes

Nutritional values: Sodium-193mg|Potassium-170mg|Phosphorus-68mg|Protein-10g|Carbs-25g|Fat-4g

Ingredients

- 1 clove of garlic

- One tiny onion

- 1 tiny zucchini

- 1 medium-sized carrot

- 2 tbsp. of olive oil

- 1 tsp. of curry powder

- 3 cups of low-sodium chicken stock

- 1/4 tsp. of salt

- 1 cup of orzo pasta, unprocessed

- 1/4 cup cheese, parmesan

- 2 tbsp. of fresh parsley

- 1/2 cup of thawed green peas

- 1/4 tsp. of black pepper

Directions

1. Chop the garlic finely. Chop the onions and the zucchini. Shred carrots,

2. Heat the olive oil in a wide skillet over medium heat. Simmer the garlic, onion, zucchini, and carrots for five min.

3. Bring curry powder, chicken stock, and salt and bring to a simmer.

4. Bring orzo pasta and whisk before the mixture comes down to a simmer. Cover and lower the heat to a boiler. Cook until the liquid is consumed and the pasta is al dente, stirring regularly for around 10 minutes.

5. Add the cheese, the sliced parsley, and the chilled peas. Heat unless the veggies are warm; add a little more broth if possible to preserve the creaminess. Add a seasoning to taste.

10. CHICKEN TERIYAKI PITA SANDWICH

Serving: 1

Preparation time: 4 hours

Nutritional values: Sodium-554mg|Potassium-359mg|Phosphorus-170mg|protein-18g|Carbs-30g|Fat-16g

Ingredients

- 7 tsp. of Kikkoman® Teriyaki Sauce (Low Sodium)

- 8 oz. uncooked boneless and skinless chicken breast

- Onion (1 cup)

- Half cup of scallions

- Half cup of lettuce

- 1/2 cup of tomato

- 2 tbsp. of extra virgin olive oil

- 1/3 cup mayonnaise (low-fat)

- Two large white pita bread, about 7 inches in diameter

Directions

1. Place the chicken in a zip-top bag and secure it. Refrigerate for 3 - 4 hours after adding 5 tsp.—teriyaki sauce.

2. Slice scallions, lettuce, and tomato; diced onion.

3. Heat up one tablespoon of oil in a moderate frying pan and sear chicken completely until no pink exists.

4. Meanwhile, sauté onion in one tablespoon olive oil in a shallow frying pan.

5. Incorporate mayonnaise, scallions, and two teaspoons of Kikkoman® Reduced Sodium Teriyaki Sauce when the chicken & onion are cooking. Set aside the mixture.

6. Cut a few strips of every cooked chicken breast.

7. Pick pita halves and fill inside with a mixture of mayonnaise. Fill a pita with chicken and a top with sautéed onions, lettuce, and tomatoes.

11. CHICKEN VERONIQUE

Serving: 1

Preparation time: 35 minutes

Nutritional values: Sodium-167mg|Potassium-543mg|Phosphorus-292mg|Protein-27g|Carbs-9g|Fat-18g

Ingredients

- 2 chicken breasts, boneless and skinless (4 oz. each)

- 2 tbsp. unsalted butter

- Half a shallot

- Cornstarch, 1 tsp.

- 2 tbsp. white wine (dry)

- 2 tbsp. chicken stock (low sodium)

- 1/2 cup green grapes (seedless)

- 1 tsp. tarragon (dried)

- 1/4 cup heavy cream

Directions

1. Heat the butter in an 8-inch pan and fry the chicken breasts on all sides unless lightly browned. Place on a plate after removing it from the pan.

2. The shallot should be finely chopped and sautéed until soft.

3. In a tiny mixing bowl, combine the cornstarch, wine, as well as broth. Drop into the pan, constantly stirring, before adding the chicken breasts. Cook for 4 - 5 minutes with the cover on.

4. Cut the grapes in half whilst the chicken is simmering.

5. Take out the chicken from the pan and keep it warm by covering it. In a large skillet, bring the cream & tarragon to a boil. Cook until the grapes are cooked through.

6. Place a chicken breast on each plate and top with sauce and grapes.

12. CEVICHE CARIBE

Serving: 1-2

Preparation time: 30 minutes

Nutritional values: Sodium-115mg|Potassium-146mg|Phosphorus-43mg|Protein-4g|Carbs-5g|Fat-3g

Ingredients

- 12 large peeled diced shrimp

- 2 onions (green)

- 1 tomato, medium

- 1 banana pepper, medium yellow

- 1 chili pepper, fresh and hot

- 2 tbsp. cilantro, chopped

- Lime juice (three tablespoons)

- 2 tbsp. white distilled vinegar

- 1 tsp. powdered garlic

- 1 cup pineapple (fresh)

- 1 tbsp. extra virgin olive oil

Directions

1. Remove the tails from the shrimp and thaw them. Cut into little bits.

2. Incorporate green onions, tomato, peppers, and cilantro into a food processor and turn on-off to grind to a very gritty consistency. The texture should be chunky. In a separate bowl, combine the lemon juice, vinegar, and garlic powder.

3. Apply the diced shrimp and the olive oil to the mix in a serving dish.

4. Peel the fresh pineapple and slice it. Place in a food processor and spin until coarsely chopped. Combine the pineapple, shrimp, and vegetables in a mixing bowl. Combine the ingredients in a mixing bowl.

5. Cook for thirty min or more when served.

3.4 Dessert Recipes

1. ORANGE AND CINNAMON BISCOTTI

Serving: 18

Preparation time: 1hr 8min

Nutritional values: **Sodium-76mg|Potassium-53mg|Phosphorus-28mg|Protein-2g|Carbs-22g|Fat-6g**

Ingredients

- 1 cup of sugar

- 1/2 cup room temperature unsalted butter

- Two eggs, large

- 2 tsp. peel of orange

- 1 tsp. of extract of vanilla

- 2 cups of flour (all-purpose)

- 1 tsp. of tartar cream

- ½ teaspoon of baking soda

- 1 tsp. of cinnamon, ground

- ¼ tsp. of salt

Directions

1. Preheat the oven to 325 degrees F.

2. Squirt two baking sheets with a nonstick cooking spray.

3. In a wide mixing bowl, mix together the sugar as well as unsalted butter until smooth.

4. One at a time, add the eggs, pounding well after each addition.

5. Blend with the orange peel plus vanilla extract.

6. In a medium-sized dish, combine flour, tartar cream, and soda for baking, cinnamon & salt.

7. Add the dry ingredients to the butter mixture and combine until blended.

8. Divide the dough in half. Put each half of it on a primed sheet. Turn each half into a 3 inch broad by 3 quarters of an inch high log with lightly floured hands. Bake for around 35 minutes until the dough logs are stable to the touch.

9. Remove the dough logs from the oven and cool for 10 minutes.

10. Move logs to the working surface. Cut on the diagonal with a serrated knife into 12-inch-thick slices. Place on baking sheets with the cut side down.

11. Bake until the bottom is golden, around 12 minutes.

12. Turn the biscotti over; cook until the bottoms are crispy, around 12 extra minutes.

13. Transfer to the wire rack and let it cool while serving.

2. VERY BERRY BREAD PUDDING

Serving: 10

Preparation time: 30 minutes

Nutritional values: Sodium-231mg|Potassium-172mg|Phosphorus-134mg|Protein-9g|Carbs-36g|Fat-23g

Ingredients

- 8 cubes of Challah bread

- 6 pounded eggs

- Thawed 12-ounce pack of chilled berry medley

- 1/2 cup of sugar

- 2 tsp. extract of vanilla

- 1 tbsp. zest of orange

- ½ tsp. of cinnamon

- Cream, whipped

Directions

1. Preheat oven to 375 degrees Fahrenheit.

2. In a wide mixing bowl, stir together the eggs, sugar, zest of orange, milk vanilla, & cinnamon unless well combined.

3. Use your hands to combine the bread cubes and berries.

4. Cover with foil and bake for 35 minutes in a buttered/greased tray. If you're going to use butter, ensure it's unsalted.

5. Remove the foil, then bake for another 15 minutes.

6. Switch off the oven & leave it for ten min.

7. Cut and serve with whipped cream on top.

3. SUNBURST LEMON BARS

Serving: 24

Preparation time: 1 hour

Nutritional values: Sodium-27mg|Potassium-41mg|Phosphorus-32mg|Protein-2g|Carbs-28g|Fat-9g

Ingredients

For crust:

- 2 cups flour (all-purpose)

- 1/2 cup sugar (powdered)

- 1 cup unsalted butter (2 sticks), room temperature

- 4 eggs as a filling

- 1/2 cup sugar

- 1/4 cup flour (all-purpose)

- Half teaspoon of cream of tartar

- ¼ tsp. of baking soda

- ¼ cup of lemon juice.

For Glaze:

- 1 cup of powdered sugar, processed

- 2 tbsp. of lime juice

Directions

For crust:

1. Preheat the oven to 350 degrees Fahrenheit.

2. Integrate the flour, sugar, and 1 cup melted butter in a wide mixing bowl. Stir until the mixture is mushy. In a 9" x 13" baking tray, press the mixture onto the bottom.

3. Bake for 15 to 20 minutes, or until golden brown.

For Filling:

1. In a moderate mixing bowl, gently whisk the eggs.

2. Integrate the sugar, cream, flour, and baking soda in a separate bowl. Combine the dry ingredients with the eggs. Whisk in the lime juice until the solution is somewhat thickened.

3. Pour over the hot crust and cook for the next 20 minutes or unless the filling is ready.

4. Take out from the oven and set aside to cool.

For Glaze:

1. Mix the lime juice into the powdered processed sugar in a tiny bowl until it's spreadable. As required, adjust the amount of lemon juice.

2. Spread the chilled filling on top. Enable the glaze to set before cutting into 24 strips. Refrigerate the remaining lemon bars.

4. LEMON GINGER CHEWY COCONUT COOKIES

Serving: 2 dozen

Preparation time: 40 minutes

Nutritional values: Sodium-40mg|Potassium-27mg|Phosphorus-17mg|Protein-1g|Carbs-11g|Fat-6g

Ingredients

- 1/2 cup butter (unsalted) (1 stick)

- 1/2 cup of sugar

- 1 beaten egg

- 1/2 teaspoon of baking soda

- Lemon juice (two tablespoons)

- 1 tablespoon lime zest

- 1 1/4 cup of flour

- 1 cup coconut flakes, toasted (unflavored)

Directions

1. Preheat the oven to 350 degrees Fahrenheit.

2. Place unflavored coconut on a baking tray and bake for 5–10 minutes or until the corners are light brown.

3. Remove from the oven and place in a mixing bowl.

4. Using an electric mixer, combine the sugar and butter until soft and fluffy. Mix in the egg,

lemon juice, ginger, and lemon zest until creamy.

5. Combine flour and the soda together. Mix the mixture of flour into the mixture of butter until it is fully combined.

6. Refrigerate for at least 30 minutes after covering.

7. Take the tablespoon-sized balls and wrap them in the sautéed coconut. Place balls on a lightly oiled baking tray about 2 inches apart.

8. Bake for 10–12 minutes, or until the edges are gently browned. Remove from the oven and set aside to cool on the counter or a cold surface.

5. DRIED CRANBERRY FRUIT BARS

Serving: 24

Preparation time: 50 minutes

Nutritional values: Sodium-34mg|Potassium-28mg|Phosphorus-34mg|Protein-2g|Carbs-31g|Fat-7g

Ingredients

For crust:

- 1 1/2 cup of flour (all-purpose)

- 1 1/3 cups of sugar

- 1 1/2 sticks unsalted butter (3/4 cup)

For Topping:

- 1/2 CUP FLOUR (ALL-PURPOSE)

- 1 tsp. powdered baking

- 1 cup cranberries, dried

- Sugar (3/4 cup)

- Four eggs

- 1 tsp. extract of vanilla

- Icing sugar for dust (optional)

Directions

1. Preheat the oven to 350 degrees Fahrenheit.

2. Whisk sugar & flour together in a moderate mixing bowl; slice out unsalted butter before mixture adheres together. Pat into a 9" x 13" baking tray that hasn't been greased. Bake for 10 minutes, or until golden brown.

3. Sift flour & baking powder together in a small bowl to prepare the topping. Toss in the cranberries that have been dried. Set aside,

4. Combine the sugar, eggs, and vanilla in a medium-sized mixing bowl. Toss in the flour mixture. Pour onto the crust that has been cooked. Bake for 20-25 minutes.

5. Slice into 24 bars when it is warm and sprinkle with icing sugar.

6. CREAM CHEESE SUGAR COOKIES

Serving: 48

Preparation time: 2-3 hours

Nutritional values: Sodium-33mg|Potassium-11mg|Phosphorus-11mg|Protein-1g|Carbs-9g|Fat-5g

Ingredients

- 1 cup of sugar
- 1 cup unsalted, melted butter
- 3 oz. melted cream cheese
- 1 large split egg
- 1/2 tsp. salt
- 1/4 tsp. extract of almond
- 1/2 tsp. extract de vanilla
- 2 1/4 cup flour (all-purpose)
- Colored sugar is an option for garnish.

Directions

1. Combine the sugar, butter, salt, extract of almond, cream cheese, vanilla extract, and egg yolk in a large mixing bowl. Mix well. Stir in the flour until it's completely combined.

2. Refrigerate cookie dough for at least 2 hours.

3. Preheat the oven to 350 degrees Fahrenheit.

4. Roll out the dough one quarter at a time to a thickness of 14 inches on a lightly floured surface. Using lightly floured cookie cutters, cut into perfect forms.

5. Put this 1 inch apart on cookie sheets that haven't been greased. Brush cookies with a gently pounded egg white and dust with colored sugar, if wanted.

6. Bake for 7–9 minutes, or until nicely golden brown. While serving, leave to cool thoroughly.

7. MOLTEN MINT CHOCOLATE BROWNIES

Serving: 12

Preparation time: 1hr 15min

Nutritional values: Sodium-147mg|Potassium-120mg|Phosphorus-61mg|Protein-3g|Carbs-36g|Fat-18g

Ingredients

- Brownie mix of Betty Crocker®, one box (not supreme)

- 12 mint chocolates from Andes®

- Powdered sugar

- Cocoa powder (unsweetened or sweetened),

- Fresh mint sprigs are all appropriate garnish options.

Directions

1. Preheat the oven to 350 degrees Fahrenheit and prepare the brownie batter according to the package instructions.

2. Prepare 12 cups of the muffin tin with a filler or finely grease & flour on the underside—Bake for 25 minutes after adding the brownie mix to the cups.

3. Remove the brownies from the oven and place one slice of mint chocolate in the middle before baking for another 5 minutes. Switch the oven off and remove. Let it cool for 5 to 10 minutes.

4. Take out brownie cupcakes from the tray and serve.

8. HONEY MAPLE TRAIL MIX

Serving: 1

Preparation time: 30 minutes

Nutritional values: Sodium-178mg|Potassium-84mg|Phosphorus-66mg|Protein-3g|Carbs-47g|Fat-9g

Ingredients

- 3 cups of Golden Grahams® cereal
- 5 cups of Rice Chex® cereal
- 10 oz. of Cinnamon Teddy Grahams® snack cookies
- 6 ounces of Pretzel Crisps®
- 1/2 cup of butter
- 1/3 cup of dark brown sugar
- 1/4 cup of honey

- 1/4 cup of maple syrup

- Five ounces of dried cranberries, flavored

- 3 ounces of Crispy Granny Smith Apple Chips®

Directions

1. In a large bowl, mix Golden Grahams, Teddy Grahams, pretzels & Rice Chex,

2. Melt butter in a tiny saucepan, incorporate brown sugar, honey & maple syrup. Process over a low flame until the sugar has dissolved.

3. Pour over the cereal mixture and blend properly before all the pieces have been coated.

4. Preheat the oven to 325 degrees F.

5. Prepare 3 jelly roll dishes, lined with aluminum foil and sprayed with cooking spray. (This can be achieved in three batches). Spread the cereal mixture uniformly over the pan. Bake at 325°F for 20 minutes, stirring halfway through.

6. Add cranberries & apple chips; shared evenly and stir.

7. Bake for five further minutes; cool thoroughly and place in an airtight bag.

9. BERRIES NAPOLEON

Serving: 1

Preparation time: 40 minutes

Nutritional values: Sodium-100mg|Potassium50mg|Phosphorus-25mg|Protein-2g|Carbs-20g|Fat-1g

Ingredients

- 12 wrappers of wontons

- 2 tbsp. sugar (granulated)

- 1 cup fat-free Reddi-Wip® whipped topping

- Half-cup raspberry

- Half cup of blueberries

- 1 tbsp. sugar (powdered)

Directions

1. Preheat the oven to 400 degrees Fahrenheit.

2. Spray a baking sheet with cooking spray large enough to hold twelve wonton wrappers.

3. Spray the wonton wrappers with cooking spray and spread them out.

4. On the wonton wrappers, slather the granulated sugar.

5. Take the wontons from the baking sheet after 5 minutes or until lightly browned.

6. On a serving tray, put six wonton wrappers.

7. Cover every wrapper with two tablespoons of whipped toppings, one tablespoon of

raspberries & 1 tablespoon of blueberries.

8. Cover the berries with a second wonton wrapper.

9. Powdered sugar can be sprinkled on top. If needed, cover them with a spoonful of whipped cream, fruit, and a mint leaf. Serve right away.

10. CHEESE TARTS

Serving: 1

Preparation time: 45 minutes

Nutritional values: Sodium-78mg|Potassium-49mg|Phosphorus-27mg|Protein-2g|Carbs-14g|Fat-8g

Ingredients

- Cream cheese, 8 oz.

- 2 egg

- Sugar, 3/4 cup

- Vanilla extract (two teaspoons)

- 2 dozen cupcake liners (paper)

- 2 dozen wafers (vanilla)

- 1 1/2 cup filling for apple pie

Directions

1. Before making the tarts, let the cream cheese soften for 1 hour.

2. Preheat the oven to 350 degrees Fahrenheit.

3. In a mixing bowl, mix cream cheese, eggs, sugar, and vanilla extract unless creamy.

4. In a muffin tray, mount cupcake liners. Top each cupcake liner with one vanilla wafer.

5. Cover vanilla wafer 3/4 completely of cream cheese mixture.

6. Oven for 10 minutes at 350°F. Remove the tarts from the oven and place them in the freezer to cool.

7. Immediately before eating, spoon 1-1/2 tbsp. Of fruit pie filling into each tart.

11. DESSERT CUPS WITH FRESH FRUITS

Serving: 1

Preparation time: 12 minutes

Nutritional values: Sodium-51mg|Potassium-83mg|Phosphorus-14mg|Protein-2g|Carbs-18g|Fat-4g

Ingredients

4 sheets of phyllo pastry dough, 14" x 18".

Butter-flavored non - stick cooking spray

1 cup of fresh blueberries

1 cup of fresh blackberries

1 cup of raspberries

1 cup of strawberries

3 cups of Cool Whip® thawed dessert icing

Directions

1. Preheat the oven to 400 degrees F.

2. Spray 12 cup muffin tray with Pam® butter-based cooking spray.

3. Layer four sheets of phyllo dough, gently coating each layer with a cooking spray. To produce dessert cups, slice phyllo dough into 3-1/2" squares and put it in the muffin pan.

4. Place the muffin pan in the oven and bake for 10-12 min or unless the phyllo cups are nicely browned. Cool at room temperature.

5. Load each phyllo dessert cup with 1/3 cup of fresh berries when ready to serve. Cover with 1/4 cup of Cool Whip cake topping.

12. FROZEN FRUIT DELIGHT

Serving: 1-2

Preparation time: 3 hours

Nutritional values: **Sodium-59mg|Potassiun-99mg|Phosphorus-36mg|Protein-1g|Carbs-21g|Fat-5g**

Ingredients

- 1/3 cup of maraschino cherries

- 8 oz. of sliced pineapple, canned

- 8 ounces sour cream (low-fat)

- 1 cup of lime juice

- 1 cup of diced strawberries

- 1/2 cup of sugar

- 1/8 tsp. of salt

- 3 cups of Reddi-Wip® dairy topping

Directions

Chop the cherries, then drain the pineapples.

Add all ingredients but the whipped topping in a medium-sized bowl and mix until well combined. Fold the whipped topping.

Place the mixture in a plastic refrigerator and freeze for 2 - 3 hours unless frozen.

Conclusion

Kidney disease (also known as renal disease) is a term used to describe when the kidneys are compromised and no longer function properly. When diagnosed, kidney disease is treatable. However, since it always goes unnoticed before severe damage has occurred, it's essential to seek medical help if you have any symptoms.

Chronic kidney disease is a condition in which the kidneys continue to worsen. If kidney damage occurs quickly—as a result of an accident or illness, for example—it is considered an acute renal failure. This can induce long-term kidney damage, even though it is just minor. To treat your chronic kidney condition (CKD), you can need to alter your diet. Create a meal plan with the help of a licensed dietitian that contains meals you love while preserving kidney health.

The RENAL diet is a simple and efficient method of maintaining a healthy lifestyle. It assists in the prevention of diseases that can affect the kidneys. If you are fresh to the RENAL diet, don't worry; it is really easy to learn and incorporate.

Your health is impacted by what you consume and drink. Maintaining a good weight and consuming a well-balanced, low-salt, low-fat diet can help you manage the blood pressure. If you do have diabetes, you may help regulate your blood pressure by consciously deciding what to eat and drink. Controlling hypertension and diabetes can help prevent the progression of kidney disease.

A kidney-friendly diet can also help in the prevention of further kidney damage. A kidney-friendly diet restricts certain nutrients to stop minerals from circulating in the body.

CPSIA information can be obtained
at www.ICGtesting.com
Printed in the USA
LVHW061921210521
688188LV00005B/429

9 781802 867640